The Rockwool Foundation Research Unit

Study Paper No. 71

The efficiency of educational production: A comparison of Denmark with other OECD countries

Peter Bogetoft, Eskil Heinesen and Torben Tranæs

University Press of Southern Denmark

Odense 2014

The efficiency of educational production:
A comparison of Denmark with other OECD countries

Study Paper No. 71

Published by:
© The Rockwool Foundation Research Unit

Address:
The Rockwool Foundation Research Unit
Soelvgade 10, 2.tv.
DK-1307 Copenhagen K

Telephone   +45 33 34 48 00
E-mail   forskningsenheden@rff.dk
web site: www.en.rff.dk

ISBN 978-87-93119-13-0
ISSN 0908-3979

August 2014

The efficiency of educational production: A comparison of Denmark with other OECD countries

Peter Bogetoft, Eskil Heinesen and Torben Tranæs

Abstract

Denmark, Norway, New Zealand, Canada and the USA are the OECD countries that spend most on education, measured in relation to GDP. Focusing in particular on upper secondary education, this paper examines whether the heavy expenditure on education in Denmark is matched by high output from the educational sector, both in terms of a large number of students enrolled in educational programmes and a high completion rate. The methodology used is to compare (benchmark) Denmark with a relevant group of countries and to calculate how much cheaper Denmark could teach the same number of students and maintain the same graduation/completion rates as today if the country could achieve the same level of cost effectiveness as its most efficient counterparts. Comparing Denmark to a group of the richest OECD countries reveals that potential savings lie between 12 and 34 percent. Figures that fall to between zero and nine percent when a comparison is made between Denmark and other Northern European countries. On the input side, the slightly weaker academic level among young people in Denmark on completion of lower secondary education – as measured by the PISA scores of the various countries – goes some way to explain the higher costs of upper secondary education. On the output side, if earnings and levels of employment among those who complete their education are taken into account, then Denmark is in fact found to be efficient. However, this high level of efficiency has become less clear-cut in recent years, since expected earnings (multiplied by rate of employment) is currently falling in comparison with the expected earnings in the peer countries. This might be an indication that Denmark's current position is not stable, unless the present situation is entirely attributable to the economic downturn in the wake of the financial crisis.

1. An international perspective is ever more important

Efficiency in education has always been important, but new dimensions will be added to its importance in the future, given that Danish firms will increasingly be able to cover their requirements for a trained workforce by employing immigrants educated in other (EU) countries, and young Danes will increasingly be able to acquire their education abroad. If a given educational programme can be taught more efficiently in countries other than Denmark – higher quality for the same or lower costs – it will no longer be possible to make the same arguments as today for having the taxpayers finance that educational programme in Denmark, at least not to the same extent as hitherto.

As is the case in other small, affluent countries, enterprises in Denmark are very internationally-oriented, and have continuously adapted themselves to the new conditions that have arisen in the wake of globalisation. The first phase of this process was the free movement of goods, which was followed by the free movement of capital, and, finally, by the phase of globalisation in which we are today: the free movement of labour. The closest integration throughout the process has taken place at regional level, in Denmark's case within the EU.

The more direct access to the entire European labour market means that firms no longer need to formulate their requirements for employees according to the qualifications of the people available locally – at least, not to as great a degree as previously. Firms less frequently have to make do with second or third best if the most suitable employees are not to be found in their country.

In terms of effects on educational policy, this new state of affairs means that the issue of which educational qualifications the Danish labour market will require in the future can increasingly be discussed independently of questions of which levels of education that the coming cohorts of Danish young people can be offered, and within which educational trajectories such levels can or should be available.

However, even if Danish firms are gradually becoming less dependent on how well young people in Denmark are educated, it remains of crucial importance for the Danish welfare state that people who grow up in Denmark are able to obtain good jobs. This requires a good education – but not necessarily a *Danish* education.

There is still no truly international market for education, but the trend is clearly moving in that direction, even for areas such as Denmark where the native language has a relatively small number of speakers. Within the Nordic region, there is a long tradition for Swedes to obtain qualifications in certain specialised fields, particularly health sciences, in Denmark, and for students from Norway and Iceland to take more general courses in Denmark. A relatively new feature is that globalisation has spread to the area of vocational training. First and foremost, this is a result of the closer integration of EU labour markets in the first decade of the new millennium – most recently through the accession of nations in Eastern and Central Europe to the Union – with the subsequent availability of large numbers of workers from the East on the labour markets of Western Europe.

While there are no indications that firms will employ fewer people with vocational qualifications in the future, the question is whether Danish firms will employ people trained in Denmark, or in other places. These developments are taking place concurrently with the long-standing efforts of the EU to harmonise educational programmes in the various member states, thus making it easier for people to take courses outside their home countries.

This makes completely new demands of the Danish educational system in general, including upper secondary education. Even though it is unlikely that many Danish young people will take complete educational programmes in other countries, and certainly not at upper secondary level, it will nevertheless be increasingly difficult in the future to justify any situation where Denmark teaches people the same types of courses as are available in other EU countries, but at a higher cost. It is also possible that Danish firms will exert less pressure for improvements to vocational training in Denmark when they can select employees from all parts of the European labour market.

This paper puts figures on the efficiency of the Danish educational sector by means of comparison with the most relevant OECD countries, i.e. the wealthier OECD countries, and more narrowly the countries of Northern Europe. The analyses focus primarily on educational efficiency at the upper secondary school level, but also take into account educational production more generally.

It is no simple task to ensure comparability of data on resources used and services provided in different countries. This may lead to the conclusions that the efficiency levels should not be compared and that only changes in the efficiency, often referred to as the productivity, can be compared. In this paper, we do not take such an extreme position. We will make cross-country comparisons of the efficiency levels and look also at the changes of these levels from 2000 to 2010. We will be careful to use data on resources and services which are as comparable as possible, but we do acknowledge that international comparisons are intrinsically difficult. Still, it is important to attempt comparisons of levels since the comparisons of changes can be rather misleading. Countries that are inefficient have two ways to improve. They can benefit from general improvements of best practices as well as from catching up to best practice. Best practice countries on the other hand can only benefit from the improvements in best practices, so called frontier shifts. It would therefore be misleading to conclude that a country with larger improvements over time is necessarily more efficient. It may just have started at a lower efficiency level.

An international comparison of efficiency is no simple matter, and the results will inevitably involve a significant degree of uncertainty. Consequently, it is not possible to present a single unambiguous and definitive answer in this paper. Rather, we present a number of estimates which, taken together, provide an impression of the situation regarding efficiency of upper secondary programmes in Denmark.

2. Various models for upper secondary education

The structure of upper secondary educational programmes varies greatly from country to country, even if we only consider Western countries. In general terms, these countries can be classified according to their adherence to either the American or the European model for upper secondary education.

The American model covers the whole of the upper secondary education level in one broad, unified and universal *high school* system. A number of countries have broad, unified systems like that used in the USA; these include the other English-speaking countries and the countries bordering the Mediterranean.

The unified school system is adapted to a labour market that demands general qualifications, and the ability to be adaptable regarding work. All students take a number of core subjects as part of their high school studies, for example English, Mathematics, General Science and Social Sciences. A degree of differentiation is applied during the programme, however, with students grouped according to their academic skills and their interests. Some trajectories are aimed at a subsequent four-year university education, while others prepare students for vocational or technical courses of two years' duration. The courses intended to prepare students for a subsequent vocational or technical programme may be taught under one roof at a vocational technical high school.

In principle, the American model offers what is essentially a common programme for all upper secondary cohorts; but in practice it has developed into a differentiated system on the basis of later choices of programmes that lead to specific qualifications or skills.

The *European Model,* which is used in countries that include the Nordic nations, Germany, Austria and Switzerland, is characterised by a split at upper secondary level into academic course programmes, which are geared towards preparation for further studies, and vocational training programmes, which lead directly to qualifications for skilled trades.

In recent times the Nordic countries have moved in the direction of a more generalised programme, although without really approaching the American system. In Sweden, for example, there has been an attempt to merge the two types of educational programme in a single system in 'unified schools'; nevertheless, the schools maintain a clear differentiation between the two trajectories, a differentiation which has been further strengthened of late. In Denmark, the general element in the vocational programmes has been increased, but the country still maintains a dual system (Markussen, 2010). If the Danish system is nevertheless moving in the direction of the American model, it is because so many young people have rejected vocational training as their first choice, preferring instead to take an academic upper secondary programme. However, a significant proportion of young people in Denmark do choose to take an upper secondary vocational training programme at a later date, sometimes after attending an academic upper secondary course for a year or more, or in some cases even after completing such a programme. Thus, the proportion of a cohort in Denmark who do at some point enrol in a vocational upper secondary programme has not fallen over the past 10 to 15 years.

One distinguishing feature of the European model is that the most academically inclined students in primary school transfer at an early point, i.e. some years before the end of compulsory schooling, to a more academically oriented secondary school, in order to prepare to take an academic upper secondary course. Similarly, the more practically oriented students transfer to a programme aimed towards a subsequent vocational upper secondary education. In the Netherlands, for example, this separation happens after year 8 of schooling; in Spain, after year 7; in Switzerland and Germany, after year 6; and in Austria, after year 4.

The Scandinavian countries are once again an exception to the general pattern, with an educational policy based on promoting a high degree of equality. Since the 1950s, then, the structure of primary and lower secondary education has been based on a unified system from pre-school up to year 9, with the emphasis on providing differentiated teaching within that unified system. Certain other European countries, for example Hungary, use a unified system as well.

Enrolment in secondary education is dependent to some extent on whether primary education is based on a unified system, or whether students are separated relatively early in primary/lower secondary school according to their academic skills and interests, which in practice creates a restricted entry to academic upper secondary education.

2.1. Vocational upper secondary education

There are significant differences in the structure of vocational upper secondary education in Europe, including the relationship between internship in companies and study in school, and the question of whether the programme qualifies students for subsequent entry to higher level courses. There are also differences in whether the administration of the system is in the hands of national or decentralised authorities. One common feature, however, is that the labour market parties are represented and have a greater or lesser degree of formalised influence in the process of laying down the structure and content of the educational programmes, so that the skills required by the labour market are actually taught in the vocational training institutions.[1]

From an educational economics point of view, the average age of students at the start of an upper secondary vocational training course and the average age at completion are of considerable interest. In this respect, Denmark is clearly at the bottom end of the scale, if early completion is a criterion for success.

The average ages at course start, arranged in order from the lowest upwards, are as follows: Austria 15.5 years, Switzerland 17.8 years, the Netherlands 18.8 years, Germany 19.8 years and lastly Denmark 21.8 years.[2] The difference is even more pronounced for the average completion age. This is as low as 19.5 years in Austria and 21.8 years in Germany, while in Denmark it is 28.1 years.[3] While it is better to take an upper secondary vocational course late than never to take one at all, that does not alter the fact that there are socioeconomic gains to be achieved in Denmark in terms of the earlier completion of vocational training.

2.2. Comparisons between countries are difficult

Differences in educational systems – not just differences between North America and Western Europe, but also within Western Europe – mean that it is difficult to make international comparisons between course programmes, just as it is difficult to compare different educational institutions within individual countries. However, it is not crucial for some of the comparisons we make that the educational programmes should be very similar. The most important thing is to ensure that the educational programmes that are compared are generally widespread within a society, so that it can be stated with reasonable certainty the extent to which people who have completed the programme in question or a given level of education then obtain employment, and at what wages, since earnings are used here as a measure of social productivity. Earnings are not a perfect measure, but in this context they form the most appropriate one available. Whether educational programmes or levels have one structure or another is less important in this context. However, the costs involved are crucial.

---

[1] DEA (2013).
[2] DEA (2013). The figures for Denmark and the Netherlands are for 2011, for Germany 2010, for Switzerland 2006 and for Austria 2009.
[3] DEA (2013). The figures are for the same years as stated in the previous note. No figures are available for the Netherlands and Switzerland.

3. Educational production: costs and output

In this section, we discuss a few key figures for the educational production of various countries. Table 1 shows the total costs for educational institutions in selected OECD countries as percentages of GDP, subdivided into private and public costs. Costs of research are included in the figures for tertiary education where the research is conducted at institutions (such as universities) that are also involved in teaching. The average consolidated cost of primary, secondary and tertiary education in OECD countries is 5.9 percent of GDP (as shown in the column farthest to the right); public and private costs represent 4.5 and 1.4 percent of GDP respectively. Denmark spends a total of 6.7 percent of GDP on education, and is thus one of the countries that spends most in this area, the others being Norway, Canada, the USA and New Zealand. In the Nordic countries, virtually all the costs fall on the public budget, while a significant part of the costs of tertiary education are paid from private sources in the USA, Japan, Australia, Canada, the United Kingdom, the Netherlands and Portugal. Even in the USA, however – the country where most private funds are spent on education – the public purse meets more than twice as much of the costs of the education system as a whole.

The first four columns in Table 2 show the costs per student in primary school, in lower secondary school, in upper secondary school, and in tertiary education. These costs are given in US dollars and are Purchasing Power Parity (PPP) corrected.[4] The table shows that Denmark (together with other countries including Norway, the USA and Luxembourg) spends relatively heavily per student in primary school, but that spending by Denmark is not particularly high for the other three levels of the education system.

The next three columns in Table 2 indicate how large a proportion of a birth cohort is expected to graduate from upper secondary school, short-cycle courses of tertiary education and medium-cycle or long-cycle courses of tertiary education. The calculation of these graduation rates involves a considerable amount of uncertainty, and the fact that education systems differ to such a great degree also means that the classification of programmes into these two types of tertiary education may be debatable. The figures indicate that Denmark, with a graduation rate of 86 percent for upper secondary education, lies at around the middle of the list of countries given, and is among the most highly-placed countries for medium-cycle and long-cycle courses of tertiary education with a 50 percent graduation rate.

---

[4] See the section on DEA models below for a more detailed discussion of the PPP correction used.

The final three columns show average earnings for given levels of education, converted to euro using PPP correction. Compared with other countries, earnings for people with only lower secondary education are very high in Denmark, as are the earnings of people who have completed upper secondary schooling (but no tertiary education); however, earnings in Denmark for people with tertiary education are not particularly high.

Table 1. Costs of educational institutions as percentages of GDP, subdivided into public and private costs (2010)

	Primary and secondary education			Tertiary education			Total		
	Public	Private	Total	Public	Private	Total	Public	Private	Total
	(1)	(2)	(3)	(4)	(5)	(6)	(7)	(8)	(9)
Denmark	4.7	0.1	**4.8**	1.8	0.1	**1.9**	6.5	0.2	**6.7**
Finland	4.1	0.0	**4.1**	1.9	0.1	**1.9**	6.0	0.1	**6.1**
Norway	5.1	0.0	**5.1**	1.6	0.1	**1.7**	6.7	0.1	**6.8**
Sweden	4.0	0.0	**4.0**	1.6	0.2	**1.8**	5.6	0.2	**5.7**
Iceland	4.7	0.2	**4.9**	1.1	0.1	**1.2**	5.9	0.3	**6.2**
The Netherlands	3.7	0.4	**4.1**	1.3	0.5	**1.7**	5.0	0.9	**5.8**
Belgium	4.3	0.1	**4.4**	1.4	0.1	**1.4**	5.6	0.2	**5.8**
United Kingdom	4.8	0.0	**4.8**	0.7	0.6	**1.4**	5.6	0.6	**6.2**
Ireland	4.6	0.2	**4.8**	1.3	0.3	**1.6**	5.9	0.5	**6.3**
Austria	3.5	0.1	**3.6**	1.5	0.1	**1.5**	5.0	0.2	**5.2**
France	3.8	0.3	**4.1**	1.3	0.2	**1.5**	5.1	0.5	**5.6**
Italy	3.1	0.1	**3.2**	0.8	0.2	**1.0**	3.9	0.3	**4.2**
Spain	3.0	0.3	**3.3**	1.1	0.3	**1.3**	4.1	0.5	**4.7**
Portugal	3.9	0.0	**3.9**	1.0	0.4	**1.5**	4.9	0.4	**5.3**
Australia	3.7	0.6	**4.3**	0.8	0.9	**1.6**	4.5	1.5	**6.0**
New Zealand	4.4	0.6	**5.1**	1.0	0.5	**1.6**	5.5	1.2	**6.7**
Canada	3.4	0.4	**3.9**	1.5	1.2	**2.7**	5.0	1.6	**6.6**
Japan	2.8	0.2	**3.0**	0.5	1.0	**1.5**	3.3	1.2	**4.5**
USA	3.7	0.3	**4.0**	1.0	1.8	**2.8**	4.7	2.1	**6.8**
OECD, unweighted averages	3.7	0.3	**4.0**	1.1	0.5	**1.7**	4.8	0.8	**5.6**
OECD, weighted averages	3.5	0.3	**3.9**	1.0	1.1	**2.1**	4.5	1.4	**5.9**
EU 21,[*] unweighted averages	3.7	0.2	**3.9**	1.2	0.3	**1.5**	4.9	0.4	**5.4**

Source: OECD (2013: Table B2.3).

[*] EU21 = all EU member states prior to the accession of ten additional countries on 1 May 2004, plus the four Eastern European member countries of the OECD, namely the Czech Republic, Hungary, Poland and the Slovak Republic.

Table 2. Costs per student, graduation rates, and earnings by levels of education (2010)

	Costs per student (in PPP-corrected USD)				Graduation rates			Earnings for the level of education (in PPP-corrected euro)		
	Primary	Lower secondary	Upper secondary	Tertiary	Upper secondary	Short tertiary	Medium and long tertiary	Lower secondary	Upper secondary	Tertiary
Denmark	11,166	11,078	10,996	18,556	86	9	50	31,949	36,975	46,287
Finland	7,368	11,338	7,739	16,569	93	0	49	29,429	29,102	38,830
Norway	11,833	12,505	14,983	19,269	87	0	42	29,315	35,515	50,309
Sweden	9,382	9,642	10,375	19,961	75	6	37	26,934	28,893	35,886
Iceland	10,099	9,778	7,934	9,939	88	2	60	19,673	29,296	33,919
Germany	6,619	8,130	11,287	15,711	87	14	30	21,447	35,441	59,726
Netherlands	7,917	11,708	11,880	17,849		0	42	26,953	34,089	51,310
Belgium	8,341			15,443				30,007	33,785	51,018
Luxembourg	16,494	19,202	19,443		70			27,826	37,746	65,685
UK	9,088	10,124	9,929	16,338	92	12	51	27,323	30,167	42,262
Ireland	8,219	11,069	12,731	16,420	94	22	47	29,229	32,826	45,100
Austria	10,080	12,442	12,737	14,257		12	30	22,153	34,411	54,434
Switzerland	10,597	14,068	17,013	21,577		16	31	29,908	39,874	64,863
France	6,373	9,111	12,809	14,642				22,609	25,556	38,203
Italy	8,669	9,165	9,076	9,562	83	1	32	23,645	31,099	41,892
Spain	7,446	9,484	11,265	13,614	80	16	30	22,334	27,020	37,415
Australia	8,328	10,273	9,916	16,074		16	50			
New Zealand	6,812	7,304	8,670	10,619		26	47			
Canada	8,262		10,340	20,932	81	29	36			
USA	11,109	12,247	12,873	29,201	77	11	38			

Sources: OECD (2012); Eurostat (2014); own calculations.

4. How can comparisons of efficiency be made?

This section presents the data and the analytical method used. We discuss the overall perspective chosen with regard to the selection of groups of countries, the levels of the educational system for which comparisons are made, the input and output variables that are used, and the limitations of the analysis.

4.1. Data description

Most of the data used in the analysis in this paper come from the OECD's database, which among other things provides the basis for the annual publication *Education at a Glance*. The data used for most of the variables are the same as those used as the basis for *Education at a Glance 2012*, but some information which was not available there has been drawn from the 2013 issue. In addition, data concerning rates of employment and earnings related to levels of education have been taken from Eurostat (2014).

4.2. Methodology

In terms of methodology, it is not self-evident how best to conduct a data-based analysis of Danish upper secondary education in an international context.

A traditional approach to comparing countries would be based on simple key figures, such as costs per student or the share of a cohort taking upper secondary level education. The key figures for Denmark can be compared with corresponding figures for the group of countries taken to be relevant for this purpose, making it possible to test, for example, whether Denmark differs significantly from other countries with respect to any of the figures in question. Such analyses based on key figures can be useful, particularly in connection with initial studies of differences and similarities among countries. However, there are at least three problems with this approach – problems which we have attempted to avoid.

Key figures provide *too narrow a perspective*. They typically focus on the relationship between only one input and one output, thus ignoring the fact that it is possible to save in terms of one input by spending more or another, or by producing less of another output. Key figures are also based on *unrealistic assumptions*, including and in particular an assumption of constant returns to scale. If, for example, we consider the costs per student for those students in a cohort who take a given examination, and compare this (consolidated) key figure for various countries, we are assuming that there are no differences between the costs for the first and the last students who take the examination. However, there will typically be a degree of saving if a large number of students take the examination. This is the reason that small countries often do not offer a full range of educational programmes. On the other hand, there may be additional costs associated with having a very large proportion of a cohort follow a given educational programme, since this may require that some students who are less well suited to the study take the course. The third evident problem with using simple key figures is that they give little indication of which countries are truly *comparable* with Denmark. The group of countries with which Denmark should be compared must therefore be selected entirely exogenously. We apply exogenous restrictions on the comparisons as well, specifically through the use of *comparison groups*, but just as important, we also work with endogenous benchmarks by requiring that the benchmark must use less of all inputs and produce more of all outputs.

Instead of using simple key figures, in this paper we use the Data Envelopment Analysis (DEA) method,[5] which is based on *best practice*. It is a method of benchmarking that involves making comparisons with best practice in all the countries concerned, and is of interest for several reasons. For example, it is relevant to know which countries Denmark might be able to learn from. In this context, all else being equal, it is naturally more useful to learn from the most efficient countries than from countries with only average levels of efficiency. Best practice can also be said to provide an upper limit for what we can reasonably expect to save in the Danish educational sector without compromising on quality. Last, but not least, best practice represents the closest we can come to economists' concept of efficiency. If the Danish educational system is to compete in a globalised world, it is not enough for it to be just reasonably good – it must be among the most efficient.

Since benchmarking models aim to estimate what is best practice, they are relatively sensitive to single observations. It is therefore important to use good outlier identification techniques, and following the principle of caution it is important to apply aggressive outlier elimination. In all the analyses in this paper, therefore, it has been decided to eliminate frontier outliers.[6] Countries which have an extraordinary impact on the efficiency of other countries are excluded from the calculations of the efficiency of those other countries.

4.3. Particular challenges involved in international comparisons

The most obvious challenges that are faced in making international comparisons of the efficiency of the educational sector are:

---

[5] For discussions of DEA and other frontier analysis methods, see, for example, Bogetoft & Otto (2011) and Bogetoft (2012). These methods have been used for efficiency evaluations of a large number of private and public institutions, including schools, universities, hospitals, military units, post offices, the police and the courts. In Denmark, the methods have been used by ministries and consultants within a variety of areas. The first applications in Denmark concerned the evaluations of research institutions and hospitals; see Jennergren and Obel (1986) and Bogetoft, Olesen and Petersen (1987).

[6] In doing this we apply two principles, which are described in detail in Bogetoft and Otto (2011: 309) and in Appendix A.

1. The calculation of resource use
2. The calculation of the production of services
3. The interactions among the various elements of the educational system

Resource use can be measured in either monetary or physical units. Physical units include FTE teacher work years, school buildings, and so on, and calculations in physical units have the advantage of removing the effects of differences in levels of prices, etc. Monetary units, on the other hand, have the advantage of allowing differences in the quality of teachers, buildings, etc. to be taken into account.

Production of services can be measured in terms of the number of students who complete an educational programme, or in terms of the scholastic level to which the school system brings these students. The latter is the most obviously relevant service goal, but it is also difficult to calculate, since it requires correction for a number of other factors that can affect students' capabilities, including the financial and educational backgrounds of their parents. Correction for such factors is, however, rather difficult even within a given country (Bogetoft and Wittrup, 2014), and goes beyond the scope of this study. We must therefore manage here with less complete measurements of the quality of education, including graduation/completion percentages, earnings after completion, etc. We also supplement these measurements with analyses of the correlations between indicators of efficiency from DEA quantitative models and relevant indicators of quality.

The challenge presented by *interactions among educational levels* relates to what students learn at various points in time in the course of their education. It is to be expected that there will be synergy effects, and that *ceteris paribus* there will be greater possibilities for achievement at higher levels in the system if the lower levels have helped students to increase their skills substantially. Since the relationships of primary, secondary and tertiary education levels to one another vary somewhat from country to country, the interactions among the levels mean that it can be problematic just to make analyses of upper secondary education in isolation. If, for example, spending on primary/lower secondary education in a country is relatively high, it can be expected that students will complete upper secondary education more easily. Consequently, we do not only analyse models restricted to the upper secondary education level, but also conduct analyses that include all three levels at once, and also use models in which the contribution made by primary/lower secondary education is measured in approximate form through PISA scores.

The challenges described above are greatest when the countries concerned are less *comparable in general*. We can therefore reduce the sources of error significantly if we limit comparisons to include, for example, only the Northern European countries, where the educational systems, levels of wages and other socioeconomic factors are relatively comparable. The disadvantage of such an approach, however, is that every reduction in the size of the comparison group reduces the potential areas for improvement that can be identified, simply because there are fewer countries in which to discover best practice. We have worked with four different groups in the analyses. For the sake of simplicity, this paper presents the results for two comparison groups, designated *All* and *Northern Europe*. The *All* group consists of Western European countries plus certain countries in the rest of the world which are reminiscent of Denmark in various ways, namely New Zealand, Australia, Canada and the USA. The *Northern Europe* group consists of the Nordic countries, Germany, the Benelux countries, the United Kingdom and Ireland (see Table 3). Note, however, that Iceland has not been included in the comparisons, since that country deviates to a very high degree from the other countries in the database used.

Table 3. Primary comparison groups

All		Northern Europe
Denmark	Austria	Denmark
Finland	Switzerland	Finland
Norway	France	Norway
Sweden	Italy	Sweden
Germany	Greece	Germany
The Netherlands	Spain	The Netherlands
Belgium	Portugal	Belgium
Luxembourg	Australia	Luxembourg
United Kingdom	New Zealand	United Kingdom
Ireland	Canada	Ireland
	USA	

4.4. Overview of the analyses

In the following, we present the results of a number of models. The next section focuses on the purely quantitative calculations on the output side. The total costs are compared here with the number of students, first for all four levels of education (primary, lower secondary, upper secondary and tertiary), and second with a focus on the secondary education levels (lower and upper secondary) alone and on upper secondary education alone. In this way, we attempt to take into account the interactions that there may be among the levels, including substitution of costs at the different levels.

In Section 6, the qualitative dimension is brought into play in various ways. The purely quantitative analyses are supplemented with an analysis which examines whether the indicators of efficiency in the DEA quantitative models are correlated with relevant indicators of quality. In addition, DEA analyses are carried out based on 'costs per head' for students enrolled combined with indicators of quality on both the input side (using the countries' PISA scores) and on the output side (using graduation rates, completion rates and levels of earnings of students who have completed the programmes weighted with the probability of their being in employment, i.e. the relevant rates of employment).

5. Costs and student numbers (quantitative efficiency)

In this section we compare the efficiencies of the various countries on the basis of purely quantitative models in which total costs are compared with total numbers of students. The numbers of students enrolled at the various levels of education are regarded as the primary drivers of costs in these models.

5.1. An illustration of the relationship between costs and number of students

Figure 1 illustrates the relationship between the number of students in upper secondary education and the total costs of upper secondary education (measured in PPP-corrected US dollars). Each dot in the figure represents the data for one country. Large countries with many students and high total costs lie on the right-hand side of the figure (and near the top), while small countries are on the left-hand side. (The USA is not included on the figure, since it is so much larger than other countries that it would be difficult to identify other data points if it was shown.) The line shows the *production frontier*, i.e. the maximum level of efficiency found, plotted on the assumption that there are non-decreasing returns to scale in educational production (i.e. that the unit costs do not increase with the number of students). New Zealand (NZ in the figure), Portugal and Australia lie on the production frontier and are thus the most cost-efficient countries. The assumption of non-decreasing returns to scale means here that the production frontier is determined by unit costs in Australia for all points to the right of and above the level of Australia. Denmark is represented by the dot positioned immediately to the right of New Zealand (with approximately the same number of students). Luxembourg is a special case because of its size, and is an *outlier* (see the next section).

Figure 1. The relationships between costs of upper secondary education and numbers of students in upper secondary education in 2010 (graphical representation of the results from Model 4)

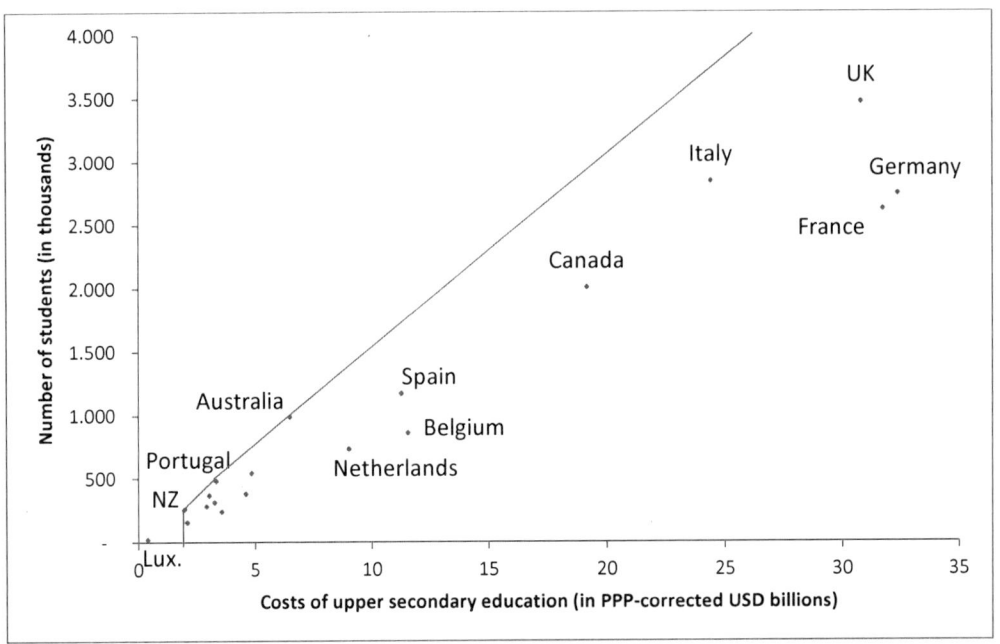

Sources: OECD (2012); own calculations.

5.2. The quantitative models

We have analysed a number of quantitative models – that is to say, models in which the numbers of students at various levels are the primary drivers of costs. Taking into account the data available and on the basis of various conceptual considerations, five models are considered to be particularly interesting. These are defined in Table 4. The first model covers the entire educational sector, while

Model 2 excludes tertiary education. Model 3 includes both lower and upper secondary levels, while Model 4 is more narrowly focused on upper secondary education. Model 5 is a supplement to Model 3 and examines the differences in the composition of the resources used in the various countries. Because of the data available, the focus here is once again on lower and upper secondary education viewed as a whole.

Table 4. Quantitative models, i.e. models where output is the number of students, and inputs are PPP-corrected costs in 2010

Model	Input: Costs	Output: Number of students
1	Total expenditure on primary, secondary and tertiary education	Primary education Lower secondary education Upper secondary education Tertiary education
2	Total expenditure on primary and secondary education	Primary education Lower secondary education Upper secondary education
3	Total expenditure on lower and upper secondary education	Lower secondary education Upper secondary education
4	Total expenditure on upper secondary education	Upper secondary education
5	Expenditure on lower and upper secondary education divided up into wages, other operating costs and capital costs	Lower and upper secondary education

Finding the best way of calculating the input side poses a considerable challenge. In this context it is important that there should be a *correspondence* between inputs and outputs – i.e. that all the resources that are used for students' schooling, and no other resources, are included on the input side. This argues for relatively highly aggregated calculations. A second challenge is to ensure that the resources are in a form that makes them directly comparable across countries. One possibility here would be to use physical units such as the number of teacher FTEs, area of school buildings, etc. However, no data are readily available on salaries, costs of buildings per square metre and the like which would make a calculation of such inputs possible on the basis of the existing statistics on expenditure. Another possibility is to work with monetary units. This enables us to measure countries not only according to their technical ability to transform given physical resources into educational yield, but also on their ability to find the cheapest mix of production factors.

The monetary accounts of costs exist in local currencies in the first instance, and must therefore be converted into a common unit. The simplest way of doing this is to use standard exchange rates to convert the costs for all countries into, for example, US dollars. However, exchange rates are very volatile, and in any case primarily reflect prices of internationally traded goods. Educational production is predominantly a local service activity, and the differences in costs of such service production can best be shown by using the Purchasing Power Parity (PPP) index. One well-known example of such a comparison concerns the prices of McDonald's hamburgers in different countries. Most of the analyses below are therefore carried out using PPP-corrected costs. There are also other options – indexing according to each country's GDP per inhabitant, for example – but for the sake of clarity, and because in our estimation it is the most suitable approach, we have decided to follow the widespread method of using PPP correction.

When the various DEA models are estimated and compared, it is apparent that for all six model specifications the best description of the data is achieved by assuming increasing returns to scale, or more accurately, non-decreasing returns to scale. This assumption means that it can be disadvantageous to be a small country, but not to be a large one. The assumption also seems to make sense, since if there are disadvantages to large-scale education systems then a country could in principle organise its education on a regional rather than a national level. Of course, it could also be argued that all countries are large enough that any disadvantages of small-scale systems could safely be ignored; however, in order to remain on the side of caution, we have decided to keep to the assumption of increasing returns to scale.

The relative efficiencies estimated in the five quantitative models for the two groups *All* and *Northern Europe* (NE) are shown in Table 5. The first row shows the unweighted averages of the efficiencies of the countries concerned.

Table 5. Relative efficiencies as estimated by the quantitative models

Quantitative model	1		2		3		4		5	
Countries	All	NE	All	NE	All	NE	All	NE	All	NE
Average	0.81	0.94	0.82	0.99	0.83	0.95	0.72	0.82	0.95	0.99
Denmark	0.63	0.90	0.66	1	0.88	0.97	0.73	0.91	1	1
Finland	0.97	1	1	1	1	1	0.87	1	1	1
Norway	0.64	0.80	0.64	0.89	0.79	0.79	0.56	0.70	0.94	0.94
Sweden	0.80	0.96	0.81	1	0.88	1	0.76	0.92	1	1
Germany	1	1	1	1*	0.89	1	0.56	0.69	1	1
The Netherlands	0.62	0.87	0.65	1	0.56	0.77	0.54	0.66	0.77	1
Belgium			1	1	1	1	0.49	0.61	1	1*
Luxembourg							1*	1*		
United Kingdom	0.85	1	0.80	1	0.86	1	0.74	0.92	1	1
Ireland	0.90	1	0.91	1	1	1	0.95	1	1	1
Austria	0.67		0.68		0.63		0.59		1	
Switzerland	0.63		0.64		0.74		0.71		1	
France	0.74		0.75		0.69		0.54		0.83	
Italy	1		0.94		0.95		0.77		1	
Spain	0.90		0.86		0.92		0.68		1	
Portugal	1		1		1		1		1*	
Australia							1			
New Zealand	1		1		1*		1			
Canada			0.90		1*		0.69		1	
USA	0.62		0.60		0.54		0.50		0.67	

*Outlier.
Source: Own calculations based on data from OECD (2012).

Let us first consider Model 1, which covers the costs of the entire education system. When Denmark is compared with the large group of countries, *All*, its relative efficiency is 0.63. This is the proportion of Denmark's current expenditure that would be needed if Denmark were to adopt the most efficient best practice from the group of comparison countries. In other words, there exists a combination of countries in the comparison group which could educate the same numbers of students as Denmark at all levels, and which could do this using costs which are lower by 1-0.63=0.37, or 37 percent.

We see that, as expected, the relative efficiency of the Danish education system declines with the size of the comparison group.[7] If Denmark is compared only with Northern Europe, the savings

---

[7] It is generally the case that a larger comparison group leads to lower relative efficiencies and thus indicates greater potential for savings. Since we eliminate any outliers, however, and a country may be an outlier in the large group while it is not one in the small group, this

potential is only 10 percent, as opposed to the 37 percent found in relation to the larger group. We also see that the potential savings for Denmark are greater than the average potential savings for the other countries when these are calculated in the same way.

The Danish potential for savings immediately appears to be considerable. It must also be remembered that this is a model with four outputs, which from a technical viewpoint is a large number in relation to the number of countries and which means that, other things being equal, all countries will have relatively high efficiency scores. Relative efficiencies normally decrease with the number of countries in the comparison group, and increase with the number of specified inputs and outputs. We see here, however, that the level for Denmark is matched only by the levels for Norway, the Netherlands, Switzerland and, to a certain degree, Austria.

When tertiary education is removed from the input and output sides, as is the case in Model 2, Denmark's position in relation to the All group does not improve noticeably; nor is there any change in the list of countries on a similar level. In contrast, Denmark's position improves considerably if we also take out primary education, as in Model 3, and focus only on the efficiency of lower and upper secondary education. In this model, Denmark's relative efficiency is above the average, even though the country could apparently save 12 percent (or 3 percent, when compared exclusively with NE countries) of its costs at this educational level. This reflects the fact, *inter alia*, that Denmark's costs are relatively high for primary education (see Table 2).

If lower secondary education is removed from the picture, as in Model 4, Denmark's position relative to other countries declines somewhat. One possible explanation for this is that lower secondary education in Denmark is relatively efficient (i.e. inexpensive), and that the costs of upper secondary education are approximately on a par with those in other countries in the All comparison group. It is also of some importance that New Zealand, which has low expenses at all levels in the educational system (see Table 2), contributes to determining the production frontier in Model 4, whereas in Model 3 it is classified as an outlier (and thus does not contribute to determining the production frontier). The data used in Model 4 and the production frontier are presented in Figure 1. A country's saving potential (and its relative efficiency score) is indicated by its (relative) horizontal distance from the production frontier. The United Kingdom, for example, spends approximately USD 31 billion, and its horizontal distance from the production frontier is around USD 8 billion. Its absolute saving potential in monetary terms is thus USD 8 billion, and relative to

---

general picture may be distorted in that the All group excluding outliers does not necessarily contain all the countries in the NE group excluding outliers. The outliers are indicated in all the models.

its actual expenditure its saving potential is 8/31 = 26 percent; in other words, its efficiency is 74 percent.

The above provisional conclusions are of course based on the assumption that the distributions of costs between primary, lower secondary and upper secondary education used by the OECD are approximately correct. However, even though it is naturally important to exercise caution about drawing conclusions concerning which parts of the Danish education system are particularly expensive in comparison with other countries, the analyses of the four quantitative models do indicate that the Danish education system as a whole is fairly costly. This is indicated in several models, even if we only compare Denmark to the average international levels, and it is indicated in all the models when comparing with best practice. The most costly levels appear to be primary, lower secondary and upper secondary education, in that order.

When we include information concerning the division of costs into wages, other operating costs and capital costs, as in Model 5, we find that relative efficiencies increase in comparison with Model 3. This is in part because there are now fewer countries in the comparison groups, because of the lack of data for some countries. It is also (and particularly) because there are now three inputs involved instead of just one. The effect of working with three inputs is that the focus is more on technical efficiency rather than efficiency in terms of costs. The difference lies in the *allocative efficiency*, i.e. the ability to select an input mix that minimises costs. Model 5 does not evaluate the ability of counties to keep total costs down by using an appropriate mix. We observe that according to Model 3, Denmark could save 12 percent of its total costs, while Model 5, in which the existing mix of wages, other operating costs and capital costs is maintained, suggests that Denmark can make no savings. There is thus evidence to suggest that one possible problem in Denmark could be with the shares of wages, other operating costs and capital costs in the total costs of education. However, it is not possible to state with certainty whether, for example, the proportion of costs allocated to wages is too large or too small, since there are countries with optimal allocative efficiency with both larger and smaller proportions of their costs spent on salaries than is the case for Denmark.

6. Explanations for the differences in efficiency in quantitative models: qualitative differences

The differences in efficiency described above may naturally be due to the fact that the models do not capture the quality of the students entering secondary education, or of those students leaving it. In this section we introduce quality as an explanatory factor, in two ways. First, we examine whether the differences in efficiency between the various countries described in the previous section correlate with important indicators of quality on both input and output sides. Next, we bring in quality indicators such as graduation/completion rates and levels of earnings among students who complete the courses as outputs in DEA analyses, where the input is costs per student (instead of using overall costs and the number of students separately as input and output respectively, as in the quantitative models described above).

The quality indicators used are:

1. Graduation rate: The proportion of a *birth cohort* who complete a given educational programme.
   - For upper secondary education: The share of a birth cohort in the population of an age typical for upper secondary education that is expected to complete upper secondary level education.
   - For tertiary education: The share of a cohort that completes a programme of tertiary education, regardless of the age at which the students complete it.
2. Completion rate: The share of *the students who start* a programme who complete it.
   - For upper secondary education: The number of students who complete a programme of upper secondary education related to the number of students who began such a programme. For some countries, a distinction is drawn between completion within the normal duration of a programme and completion within the normal duration plus two years.
   - For tertiary education: The number of students who complete a tertiary programme of education related to the number of students who began such a programme (regardless of whether completion was within the normal time, and of whether a student completed a different programme than that which he or she started initially).
3. Expected earnings after completion of an educational programme
   - This indicator is calculated for upper secondary students as a weighted sum of earnings for three groups:
     - Those who do not complete a programme of upper secondary education and who thus leave the educational system with no qualification higher than compulsory schooling

- Those who complete upper secondary education, but who do not complete tertiary education
- Those who complete both upper secondary education and tertiary education

The weights are the proportions of these three groups represented among upper secondary students.

4. Expected earnings after completing the educational programme, corrected for expected rate of employment.
    - This indicator is calculated in the same way as above, but the earnings for the three groups are multiplied by the relevant rate of employment for each group. In this way, the indicator takes into account the facts that the level of education affects both future earnings and future employment, and that those who, for example, achieve a high level of education, but are not in work, do not earn any wages. The indicator thus takes into account any trade-off that may exist between high earnings and a high rate of employment.

The point of these indicators is that, *ceteris paribus*, they can signal a high level of quality in a country's system of education if a large proportion of a birth cohort completes upper secondary education and tertiary education, if a large proportion of those who begin an educational programme also complete it, and if those who complete the programme obtain high earnings and readily find employment. The earnings used in the calculation of the last two indicators are PPP-corrected, as are the costs (see above).

The data and the methods of calculating the indicators are described in detail in Appendix B. It must be emphasised that there is significant uncertainty associated with the calculation of these indicators of quality, and that the methods of calculation and the quality of the data vary from country to country. Similarly, educational systems are to some extent structured differently in different countries. In consequence, the results of these analyses must be interpreted with caution.

6.1. Correlations between quantitative efficiency and indicators of quality

In an initial attempt to examine the significance of quality, we compared the calculated efficiency scores with a number of indicators of quality. We did this by regressing the efficiency scores on the quality indicators (one at a time) using the Tobit model, which takes account of the fact that the dependent variables (the efficiencies) are truncated (have values between 0 and 1).

In this way, we conducted analyses for 25 variables from the OECD database. In addition to the four types of quality indicator described above, we used variables that could shed light on possible differences on the input side (length of teacher training for various educational levels, and students' PISA scores). We also examined whether efficiency was correlated with per capita GDP, since one hypothesis might be that countries with high levels of productivity (high GDP per capita) also have high wage costs in the educational sector (producing low efficiency), because the educational sector has to compete for personnel with the highly productive private sector (Baumol's cost disease).

In general, there are few significant correlations. This is not entirely surprising given the limitations of the data, including the lack of data for quality indicators for some countries. If we first consider the quality variables that can be part of the input, we would expect that higher quality would be positively correlated with efficiency; but neither the length of teacher training nor PISA scores (which indicate students' scholastic level at the end of lower secondary school) produced significant correlations with efficiency.

On the output side, we might expect that higher quality would require increased costs. That would mean, for example, that a higher completion rate – i.e. a lower dropout rate – could make the teaching more expensive, leading to a lower level of efficiency. We used eight different measurements for completion rates in upper secondary education, and calculated correlations for each of them with the efficiencies calculated in each of the five models. Only in two of these 40 estimations was the correlation found to be significant, and the sign was different in the two cases. Furthermore, one of the correlations became non-significant if we controlled for GDP per capita in the regression. There are no significant correlations between efficiency and the completion rates for tertiary education, nor between efficiency and graduation rates for upper secondary education. If instead we measure the quality of education at upper secondary level by the share of a birth cohort who later go on to complete tertiary education, there is an indication that higher quality and greater cost efficiency may tend to go hand in hand (there is a significant positive correlation in two of the 15 estimations, in both cases for the efficiency estimates in Model 4). Thus, there are no grounds to suppose that the original models will show too great a potential for savings because of the failure to take into account students' level of preparedness for tertiary education. If quality is measured by level of earnings after completion of a programme, a negative effect is found in Quantitative Model 1. In other words, the countries where education is relatively expensive are also the ones where the expected earnings on completion of upper secondary education are high. The findings related to this indicator could suggest that part of the additional expenditure in some countries goes to increasing the quality of the education. However, this correlation is not found when we control for GDP per capita, nor when earnings are corrected for rate of employment (regardless of whether we control for GDP per capita or not).

GDP per capita seems to be negatively correlated with efficiency (this is the case in three of the five models), indicating that education is generally relatively expensive in countries where productivity is high. Using GDP per capita can, as mentioned previously, capture the effects of GDP on wages; countries with high GDP per capita may have high wages in the educational sector as well, without the sector necessarily being especially productive (Baumol's cost disease).

Overall, these post-analyses of quantitative efficiencies seem to show that the findings that there are potential savings to be made are relatively robust. There is little to suggest that the greater efficiency in some countries is achieved by a reduction in quality. In this context it should be noted that we have tested 25 variables in each of the five models, and for this reason alone we would expect to find a certain number of false significances.[8]

6.2. The relationship between costs per student and indicators of quality

In this section we present the variations among countries in the relationships between costs per student and indicators of quality in upper secondary education and the educational system as a whole. We focus on the four indicators of output quality described above (graduation rates, completion rates, expected earnings after completing a programme of education and expected earnings corrected for rate of employment).

In this section and the next we examine the relationships between the quality indicators and the expenditure of resources in the educational system measured as average costs per student. It is natural to hypothesise that, for example, the completion rate for upper secondary education programmes might be particularly strongly affected by expenditure per student enrolled, though at the same time the quality of lower secondary education might also have an impact. The quality of lower secondary education can be taken into account by considering either costs per student at that level or an indicator of students' scholastic level at the end of lower secondary education (which we do in some analyses by including PISA scores). We test a number of combinations of input and output in the analyses.

Figure 2 displays the correlations between the graduation rate for upper secondary education (i.e. the proportion of a birth cohort who complete an upper secondary programme) and average expenditure per student enrolled in primary and secondary education for those countries where the relevant data are available. There are very high graduation rates (over 90 percent) in Ireland,

---

[8] Since we tested for significance at the five percent level, we can predict statistically that we will find significance in six (5%*25*5) cases, even if there is in fact no true correlation. We found significance in five instances.

Finland and the UK, while Denmark – with 86 percent – is roughly on a par with Germany and Norway. Sweden's rate is 75 percent. Luxembourg has by far the highest costs per student and the lowest graduation rate, but this is largely attributable to the size of the country. Denmark has the third highest level of costs per student (after Luxembourg, Norway and the USA), while Finland has the lowest. The figure also presents the results from a DEA model based on these data by indicating the production frontier. This will be explained in more detail in the next section, as will the production frontiers shown in Figures 3-5, which are discussed below.

Figure 3 shows the relationships between completion rates (within the normal time) for upper secondary education and the costs per student enrolled. Once again, Luxembourg has the highest costs, and Finland the lowest. Ireland and the USA have the highest completion rates (at around 85 percent). In Denmark, the completion rate is relatively low (60 percent), while the costs per student are close to the average.

Figure 4 shows the relationship between expected future earnings for students in upper secondary level and average costs per student in primary and secondary education combined. Among the seven countries for which we have data for these variables, Denmark has the second highest costs per student (after Norway), but also the highest expected earnings. Figure 5 is equivalent to Figure 4, except that expected earnings are corrected for the expected rate of employment. Once again, Denmark ranks first with respect to output, followed by Norway and Sweden. In comparison with Figure 4, Sweden has now 'overtaken' the UK, Finland and Ireland, reflecting the higher rate of employment in Sweden. The expected earnings are lower for Denmark, Ireland and Spain when the 2012 rate of employment is used for the correction rather than the average rate of employment for 2007-12, but there are no great differences for Finland, Sweden, Norway and the UK when this alternative correction is applied. This is because the recession affected employment more strongly in Denmark, Ireland and Spain than in the other countries shown here. The production frontiers in Figures 4 and 5 will be discussed in the next section in connection with the results for Models 25 and 26.

Figure 2. Relationships between graduation rates for upper secondary education and costs per student in primary and secondary education in 2010

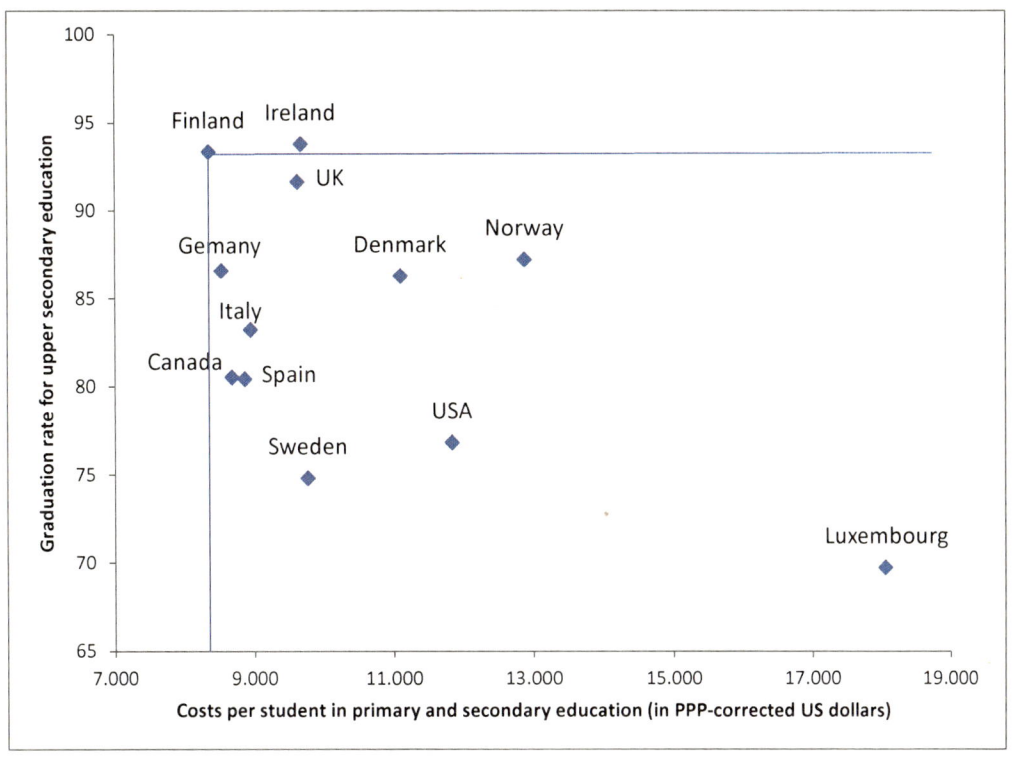

Sources: OECD (2012); own calculations.

Figure 3. Relationships between completion rates and costs per student in upper secondary education in 2010, where the completion rate is the share of the students who start a programme who complete the programme within the normal time

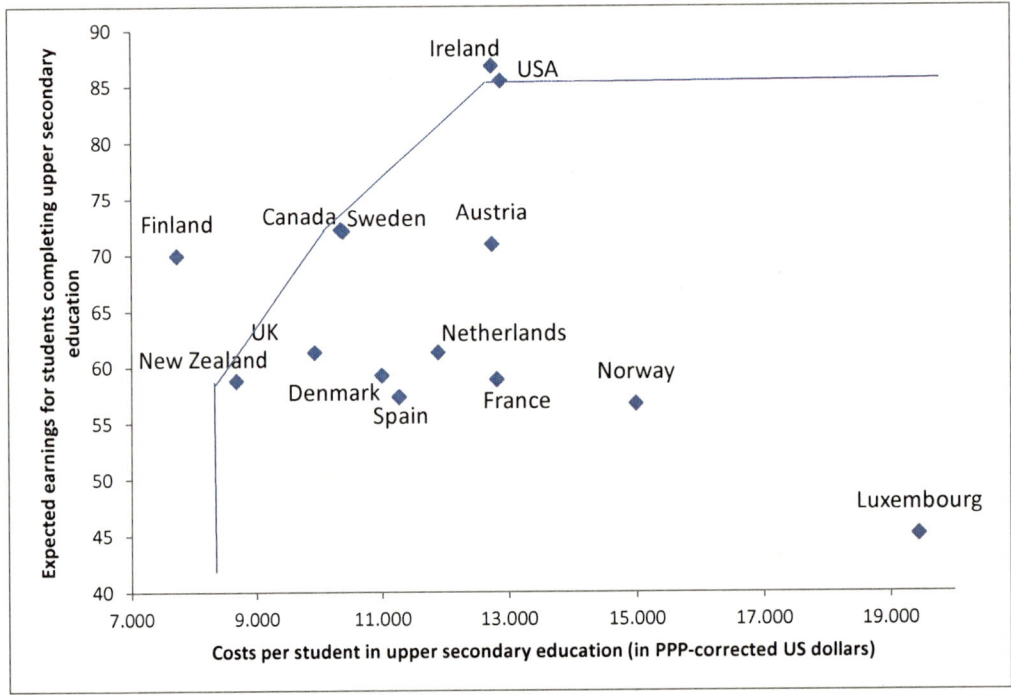

Sources: OECD (2012 and 2013); own calculations.

Figure 4. Relationships between expected future earnings (conditional on employment) for students in upper secondary education and average costs per student in primary and secondary education in 2010. Expected future earnings are calculated for various educational levels as annual earnings in 2010 for the employed.

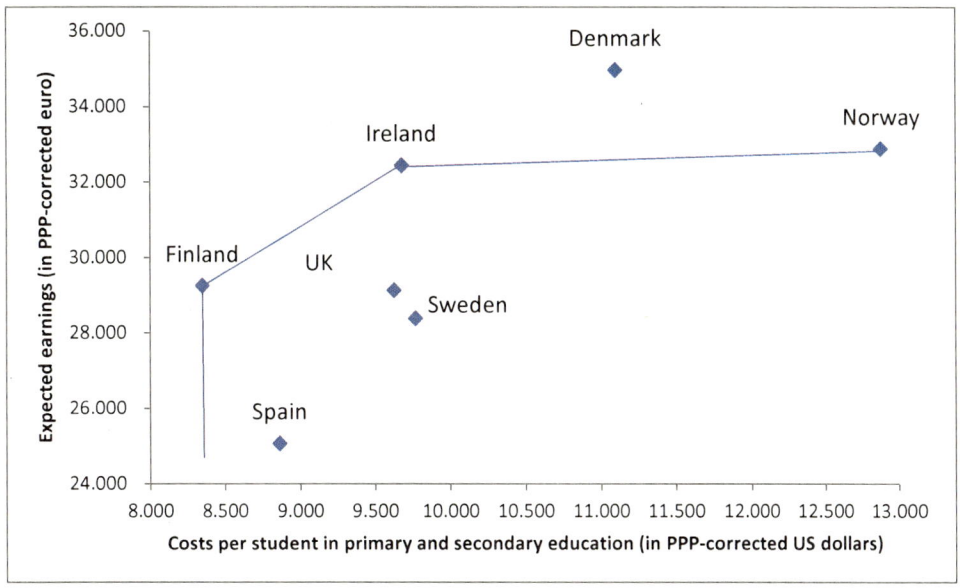

Sources: OECD (2012 and 2013); Eurostat (2014); own calculations.

Figure 5. Relationships between expected future earnings for students in upper secondary education and average costs per student in primary and secondary education in 2010. Expected future earnings are calculated for various educational levels as annual earnings in 2010 multiplied by rate of employment in both 2007-12 (average) and in 2012

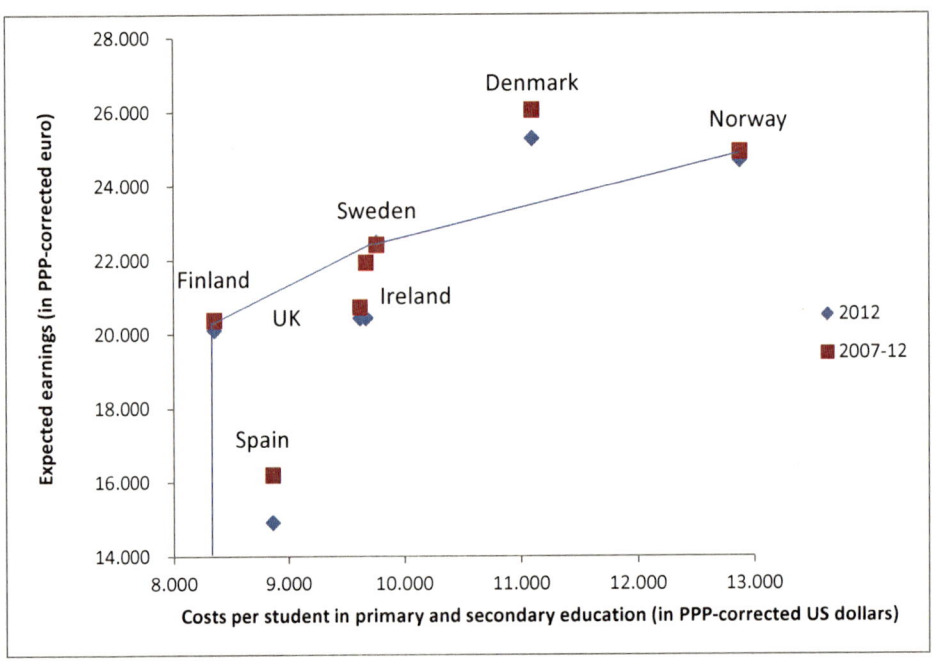

Sources: OECD (2012 and 2013); Eurostat (2014); own calculations.

6.3. DEA analyses of the relationship between quality and expenditure of resources

This section presents the results from DEA models with the quality indicators described above as outputs. Data are available from only a few countries for some of the quality indicators. It is therefore necessary to limit the number of other variables in the DEA analyses. We focus on costs per student (defined in relation to various elements of the education system) as our central input. This means that we assume constant returns to scale in the relationship between total costs and numbers of students. This is a reasonable assumption when comparing countries, since the numbers of students are large in all countries. In addition, we have aggregated parts of the educational system, in that, for example, costs per student in primary and secondary school are represented by a single aggregate variable (total costs of primary and secondary education divided by the total number of students) instead of two variables (costs per student in primary/lower secondary education and costs per student in upper secondary education). In the analyses where output is graduation or completion rates, we consider models with various different specifications of costs per student (for the entire education system, for primary and secondary education combined, for secondary education, and for upper secondary education alone).

While an assumption of non-decreasing returns to scale was made in the quantitative models described above, the models in this section were estimated using a less restrictive assumption (variable returns to scale) that allows for both increasing and decreasing returns to scale, which is appropriate given that the output comprises qualitative indicators (see the section concerning method above). As previously, we focus on input-oriented efficiency, in that a country's efficiency score reflects the proportion of its current input that would be necessary to produce its current output if it were as efficient as the most efficient comparison countries. When we permit variable returns to scale, the country with the highest level of output will be identified as being an outlier, since that country would be able to use any amount of resources (costs per student) as input and its score would still not be dominated by that of any of the other countries. This means that the relative efficiencies estimated for other countries are not affected by the country with the greatest output.

6.3.1. Graduation rates

Table 6 provides an overview of six models with graduation rates as output. Model 6 includes all levels in the education system from primary to tertiary education, with outputs being the graduation rates for upper secondary education, short-cycle tertiary education programmes, and medium-cycle and long-cycle tertiary education programmes. The other models in the table focus on graduation rates for upper secondary education as output, with inputs limited to costs per student in primary and secondary education together or upper secondary education alone. There are two outputs in Model 10, with a distinction made between graduation rates for academic and vocational upper secondary education programmes. The final model (Model 11) includes average PISA results in reading skills and mathematics as an additional input, these being indicators of the scholastic skills that students have acquired in primary and lower secondary education; such skills may have significant effects on the probability of students' completing upper secondary programmes.

Table 7 presents the DEA estimates of countries' relative efficiencies for each of the six models. It should be noted that Ireland is an outlier in all the models, because Ireland has the highest graduation rates for upper-secondary education (see Figure 2) and short-cycle tertiary education.

In Model 6, the UK and Finland are also outliers. The UK has the highest graduation rates for medium-cycle and long-cycle tertiary programmes,[9] while Finland has a combination of low costs per student and high values for output, which means that the relative efficiencies calculated for other countries are highly dependent on whether or not Finland is included in the calculation.

In Model 6 all countries are totally efficient except the USA and Sweden. This reflects the fact that the model contains many variables (four) in relation to the small number of countries that can be included (ten in the first column and seven in the second). Models 7-11 focus solely on graduation rates in upper secondary education. In Model 7, where the input is costs per student in primary and secondary education, the production frontier is determined by Finland, since Finland has the lowest costs and the highest output (apart from Ireland, which is an outlier). The results for this model are presented in Figure 2. The analyses indicate that Denmark could save (at least) 25 percent of its costs without reducing the graduation rate if the country were to become as efficient as Finland. Only Norway, the USA and Luxembourg are less efficient than Denmark. The relative potential for savings is somewhat less, however, if the input is narrowed to costs per student in secondary education only or in upper secondary education only, as seen in Models 8 and 9; these models indicate that Denmark's potential savings are 19 and 5-10 percent, respectively. When the graduation rates for all upper secondary programmes are replaced with the graduation rates for academic programmes and vocational training (as in Model 10), Denmark is found to have a relative efficiency of 0.87, or of 1 if the model is estimated only for Northern European countries. When PISA results are included as input, almost all countries are totally efficient or nearly so (again reflecting the problem with having many variables and few countries in the model).

---

[9] The graduation rates are calculated by comparing the number of students who complete a given level of education (in this case, medium-cycle and long-cycle tertiary education programmes) with the total number of people in the population in the relevant birth cohort. The UK has many foreign students, so that it is not surprising that the graduation rate is very high in proportion to the population. The OECD also has graduation rate data corrected for foreign students, but only for a very few countries. There is no corresponding problem of large numbers of foreign students as far as upper secondary education is concerned.

Table 6. Models where the output is graduation rate measured as the share of a birth cohort of a relevant age that completes a programme of education

Model	Input: Costs per student	Output: Graduation rate
6	Primary, secondary and tertiary education	Upper secondary education
		Short-cycle tertiary education[1]
		Medium-cycle or long-cycle tertiary education[1]
7	Primary and secondary education	Upper secondary education
8	Secondary education	Upper secondary education
9	Upper secondary education	Upper secondary education
10	Upper secondary education	Academic upper secondary education
		Vocational upper secondary education
11	Upper secondary education	Upper secondary education
	Additional input: PISA reading skill scores	
	PISA mathematics scores	

[1] Short-cycle tertiary education is equivalent here to Tertiary B in the OECD's database, while medium-cycle and long-cycle tertiary education are equivalent to the OECD category Tertiary A.

Table 7. Relative efficiencies from models where the output is graduation rate measured as the share of a birth cohort that completes an education. Calculated for All countries (All) and Northern European countries (NE)

Model	6		7		8		9		10		11	
Countries	All	NE	All	NE	All	NE	All	NE	All	NE	All	NE
Average	0.96	0.99	0.84	0.82	0.85	0.83	0.84	0.86	0.85	0.93	0.99	1.00
Denmark	1	1	0.75	0.75	0.81	0.81	0.85	0.90	0.87	1	0.99	0.99
Finland	1*	1*	1	1	1	1	1*	1*	1*	1*	1*	1*
Norway	1	1	0.65	0.65	0.64	0.64	0.63	0.66	0.65	1	0.98	0.99
Sweden	0.90	0.94	0.85	0.85	0.89	0.89	0.87	0.96	0.87	1	0.98	1
Germany	1	1	0.98	0.98	0.96	0.96	0.83	0.88	0.81	0.94	0.98	0.99
The Netherlands									1	1		
Luxembourg			0.46	0.46	0.46	0.46	0.47	0.51	0.47	0.53	1	1
UK	1*	1*	0.87	0.87	0.89	0.89	1	1			1	1
Ireland	1*	1*	1*	1*	1*	1*	1*	1*	1*	1*	1*	1*
Austria									0.86			
Switzerland									0.63			
France									0.82			
Italy	1		0.93		0.98		1		1		1	
Spain	1		0.94		0.88		0.81		0.83		1	
Australia									1			
Canada			0.96		0.99		0.88		1*		0.93	
USA	0.68		0.71		0.71		0.71				0.99	

*Outlier

Source: Own calculations based on data from OECD (2012).

6.3.2. Completion rates

Table 8 provides an overview of the models in which the output is completion rates in relation to the number of students who begin an educational programme. The structure of the models is approximately as in Table 6, except that in this case we estimate two versions of each model, one in which only completion of upper secondary studies within the normal time is counted, and one which includes completion in normal time plus two years. Table 9 shows the results found for the first of these specifications (completion within normal time). In the first model (Model 12), in which the output is completion rates for both upper secondary and tertiary education, Denmark is an outlier (i.e. completely efficient), because Denmark has the highest expected completion rate in tertiary education. Norway in particular, but also the Netherlands and the UK, are found to be inefficient in this model.

In Models 14, 16 and 18, where the only output is upper secondary education completion rates, Denmark's relative efficiency is fairly low (between 0.68 and 0.87) – this is lower than the efficiencies of Sweden and Finland, but higher than that of Norway. The results for Model 18 are presented in Figure 3. If a distinction is made between completion rates for academic and vocational programmes (Model 20), Denmark is completely efficient, but it should be noted that there are very few countries in the analysis (and one additional output). If PISA results are included (Model 22) then all countries have relative efficiencies that are close to 1.

Table 10 shows the results obtained if completion of an upper secondary programme is counted as long as it is within the normal duration of the programme plus two years. There are slightly fewer countries in these estimates, but for the majority of countries, including Denmark, the results closely resemble those in Table 9.

It is a general problem in this context that while we would ideally like to include many inputs and outputs in the analyses, there are relatively few countries which it is relevant to compare with Denmark and for which the necessary data are available. In a DEA analysis, where the underlying assumptions about the production process are not restrictive, virtually all countries will be categorised as efficient if the number of inputs and outputs is high relative to the number of countries. This being the case, we cannot tell whether the fact that Denmark appears to be very inefficient in many of the simple models with few inputs and outputs is due to the fact that Denmark really is inefficient, or to the fact that the models are very simple, with many factors that are not taken into account.

Table 8. Models where the output is completion rates, measured as the share of the students who begin an educational programme who go on to complete it

Model	Input: Costs per student	Output: Completion rate
12 and 13	Primary, secondary and tertiary education	Upper secondary education
		Tertiary education
14 and 15	Primary and secondary education	Upper secondary education
16 and 17	Secondary education	Upper secondary education
18 and 19	Upper secondary education	Upper secondary education
20 and 21	Upper secondary education	Academic upper secondary education
		Vocational upper secondary education
22 and 23	Upper secondary education	Upper secondary education
	Additional input: PISA reading skill scores	
	PISA mathematics scores	

Note: In Models 12, 14, 16, 18, 20 and 22 the completion rate for upper secondary programmes is measured as completion within normal time, whereas in Models 13, 15, 17, 19, 21 and 23 it is measured as completion within normal time plus two years.

Table 9. Relative efficiencies from models where the output is student completion rates measured as the share of the students who begin an education programme who go on to complete it. Calculated for all countries (All) and Northern European countries (NE). Only completion within the normal duration of the programme is counted

Model	12		14		16		18		20		22	
Country	All	NE	All	NE	All	NE	All	NE	All	NE	All	NE
Average	0.93	0.95	0.83	0.90	0.81	0.82	0.84	0.76	0.89	0.89	0.99	0.99
Denmark	1*	1*	0.68	0.87	0.72	0.81	0.79	0.70	1	1	0.98	0.99
Finland	1*	1*	1	1*	0.99	1	1*	1	1*	1*	1*	1*
Norway	0.58	0.76	0.58	0.75	0.57	0.64	0.58	0.52	0.76	0.76	0.97	0.99
Sweden	1	1*	0.89	1	0.89	1	1	1	1*	1*	1*	1*
The Netherlands	0.83	0.92	0.77	0.96	0.69	0.76	0.76	0.65	1	1	0.95	0.97
Belgium	1	1	0.84	0.99	0.81	0.83						
Luxembourg			0.41	0.53	0.41	0.46	0.45	0.40	0.57	0.57	1	1
UK	0.90	1	0.80	1	0.81	0.89	0.90	0.78			1	1
Ireland			1*	1*	1*	1*	1*	1*			1	1
Austria			0.72		0.71		0.80				1	
France	1		0.84		0.74		0.68		0.93		0.97	
Spain			0.85		0.79		0.77				1	
New Zealand	1		1		1		1				1	
Canada			1		1		1				1	
USA	1*		1		1		1				1	

*Outlier

Table 10. Relative efficiencies from models where the output is student completion rates measured as the share of students who begin an education programme who go on to complete it. Calculated for all countries (All) and Northern European countries (NE). Completion within the normal duration of the programme plus two years is counted

Model	13		15		17		19		21		23	
Countries	All	NE	All	NE	All	NE	All	NE	All	NE	All	NE
Average	0.93	0.91	0.86	0.80	0.85	0.81	0.87	0.84	0.97	1.00	0.99	0.99
Denmark	1*	1*	0.72	0.75	0.77	0.81	0.85	0.90	1	1	0.98	0.99
Finland	1	1	1	1	1	1	1*	1*	1*	1*	1*	1*
Norway	0.64	0.71	0.61	0.65	0.61	0.64	0.62	0.66	0.79	1	0.97	0.98
Sweden	0.86	0.87	0.85	0.85	0.88	0.89	0.95	0.96	1*	1*	0.99	1
The Netherlands	0.84	0.86	0.82	0.83	0.75	0.76	0.82	0.84	1*	1*	0.95	0.97
Belgium	1*	1*	1	1*	1	1*						
Luxembourg			0.44	0.46	0.44	0.46	0.49	0.51	1	1	1	1
UK	0.93	0.94	0.87	0.87	0.89	0.89	1	1			1	1
France	1*		0.97		0.88		0.84		1		0.97	
Spain			1		0.96		1				1	
New Zealand	1		1		1		1				1	
USA	1*		1*		1*		1*				1*	

*Outlier

Source: Own calculations based on data from OECD (2012 and 2013).

6.3.3. Expected earnings

Table 11 shows the results found when output is expected earnings after completion of an educational programme for students in upper secondary education, and input is the average costs per student in primary and secondary education. Even though there is only one input and one output, very few countries can be included, on account of a lack of data. Model 24 calculates expected future earnings without taking into account expected future rates of employment. These expected earnings are, as described above, a weighted average of annual earnings in 2010 for various levels of education. The output in Model 25 is expected earnings corrected for expected rate of employment. The expected earnings are thus the weighted averages of annual earnings in 2010 for various levels of education multiplied by the rates of employment for these levels of education. Rates of employment vary greatly from year to year, and we have therefore based our calculations both on average rates of employment for various levels of education in 2007-2012 and on rates of employment for 2012 alone. Denmark is an outlier in these estimates, because the expected earnings are higher than for other countries, and this also applies when a correction is made for rate of employment (though to a lesser degree when this correction is based on the rate of employment for 2012 than when it is based on an average over the years 2007-12). Finland and Norway are also completely efficient in this context, as is Sweden when correction is made for employment rate. The data underlying the results are shown in Figures 4 and 5.

Table 11. Efficiency scores for models where the output is earnings in 2010 or earnings in 2010 multiplied by rate of employment in 2007-12, and where the input is costs per student in primary and secondary education in 2010. Both inputs and outputs are PPP corrected. Calculations are made for a countries (All) and for Northern Europe (NE)

Model	24		25	
Output	Earnings		Earnings × rate of employment	
Countries	All	NE	All	NE
Average	0.95	0.95	0.97	0.98
Denmark	1*	1*	1*	1*
Finland	1	1	1	1
Norway	1	1	1	1
Sweden	0.85	0.85	1	1
UK	0.87	0.87	0.89	0.89
Ireland	1	1	0.97	0.97
Spain	0.94		0.94	

*Outlier

Source: Own calculations based on data from OECD (2012 and 2013) and Eurostat (2014).

6.4. Conclusions concerning qualitative indicators

In the models which only take into account graduation or completion rates for upper secondary education and costs per student, the estimated potential savings for Denmark are 10-32 percent, depending on the definitions used of graduation/completion rates, cost, and the comparison group. Here, then, Denmark is found to be no more efficient than in the purely quantitative models. When countries' PISA scores are included, countries such as Denmark, Norway and Sweden, which perform relatively poorly on the PISA tests, make up ground on countries such as New Zealand and Finland, which perform well, and the differences in relative efficiency are then rather small. There is, however, a problem with these analyses, in that the small number of observations relative to the number of variables tends to increase the estimates of relative efficiency. Denmark is found to be completely efficient in analyses where expected earnings after completion of educational programmes are included, if expected earnings and employment rates are based on figures for recent years.

Not many DEA analyses exist that focus on international comparisons of upper secondary education. Verhoeven, Gunnarsson and Carcillo (2007) conducted a DEA analysis of the relationship between PPP-corrected costs per student in lower and upper secondary education on the one hand and graduation rates on the other, basing their research on data from *Education at a Glance 2006*. They included more countries in their analysis, including Eastern European countries, and their results indicate that Denmark's potential savings are very considerable (2007: Figure 6). If, however, the comparison countries are limited to the same group that we have included, their results are approximately the same as ours, indicating a savings potential of around ten percent. Verhoeven, Gunnarsson and Carcillo (2007) also contains a corresponding analysis for tertiary education, which indicates that Denmark lies far from the production frontier. Afonso and Aubyn (2005) carried out a DEA analysis where the focus was on the last year of lower secondary school. The output used was PISA scores, and the inputs were the number of teachers per student and time devoted to teaching. In this analysis, Denmark ranks eleventh among 17 OECD countries, with a potential for savings of around 14 percent. In a similar analysis with corrections for GDP per capita and parents' education (Afonso and Aubyn 2006), Denmark's relative efficiency is even lower.

7. Robustness check: analyses for previous periods

As discussed above, the results concerning the relative efficiencies of various countries must be interpreted with caution. One reason is that the analyses are based on data for a single year, namely 2010 (though with some supplementary data for 2011 for completion rates). The costs in that year are compared with the numbers of students in the same year, and costs per student are compared with quality indicators such as graduation rates and expected earnings in that same year. However, student numbers in upper secondary education can vary over time in any given country, as can costs; consequently, the relationship between costs and number of students is also variable. The analyses described above of the relationship between costs and quality indicators implicitly assume that inputs and outputs remain relatively stable over time for a given country. For example, it can reasonably be assumed that the completion rate for upper secondary education in a given year is actually linked to the resources expended on the students concerned both in that year and in the previous three or four years, and to the resources expended in primary/lower secondary school even further back in time. Similarly, the earnings which students who complete such courses can expect depend on the quality of the educational system over many previous years. It is very difficult (not to say impossible) to perform satisfactory analyses that take this time element into account, since data would be missing for many countries for some of the relevant years. Instead, we describe in this section the results of a more modest robustness check, in which we conduct analyses for the period around the year 2000 instead of the period around 2010 used in the main analysis. Naturally, we have been obliged to limit these additional analyses to the models for which the key data are available for the year 2000 or around that time.

7.1. Quantitative DEA models for the year 2000

Table 12 presents the results for the first four quantitative models, calculated for the year 2000. A comparison with Table 5 indicates that Denmark's relative efficiency in the year 2000 was lower than in 2010. Using Northern European countries as the comparison group, Denmark's relative efficiency was substantially lower in 2000 compared to 2010 in all four models. Using the larger comparison group, Denmark's relative efficiency was also substantially smaller in 2000 than in 2010 for Model 3 (where input is the total costs for lower and upper secondary education, and output is the total number of students in lower and upper secondary education; see Table 4) and a little smaller in Model 1 (where input is the total costs for primary, secondary and tertiary education, and output is the total number of students in the four levels of the education system), whereas it is a little larger in models 2 (primary and secondary education) and 4 (only upper secondary education). Thus, for the larger comparison group, Denmark's improved relative efficiency from 2000 to 2010 seems driven by lower secondary and tertiary education.

Table 12. Relative efficiencies for Quantitative Models 1-4, based on data for 2000

Model	1		2		3		4	
Countries	All	NE	All	NE	All	NE	All	NE
Average	0.82	0.92	0.79	0.93	0.79	0.84	0.77	0.82
Denmark	0.59	0.73	0.72	0.74	0.56	0.56	0.76	0.76
Finland	1	1	1	1	0.89	0.89	1	1
Norway	0.63	0.83	0.79	0.84	1	1	0.85	0.85
Sweden	0.83	0.87	0.72	0.88	0.93	0.93	0.89	0.96
Germany	1	1	1	1	0.88	0.88	0.58	0.63
The Netherlands	0.67	0.96	0.62	0.99	0.63	0.63	0.66	0.71
Belgium	1	0.89	0.88	0.91			0.51	0.55
UK	1*	1	1*	1			0.81	0.88
Ireland	1	1	1*	1	1	1	1*	1*
Austria	0.66		0.57		0.57		0.68	
Switzerland	0.66		0.62		0.64		0.81	
France	0.76		0.66		0.60		0.58	
Italy	0.87		0.73		0.74		0.70	
Greece	1*		1				0.68	
Spain	1		0.94					
Portugal	1		0.89		0.98		1	
Canada	0.59		0.63					
USA	0.50		0.50					

*Outlier

Source: Own calculations based on the OECD database used in connection with *Education at a Glance*.

7.2. DEA models with qualitative indicators for 2000

Table 13 shows the results for Models 7, 8 and 9, in which the output is the graduation rate for upper secondary education in 2003 (since no data are available for earlier years) and the inputs are costs per student in 2000 for primary and secondary education, secondary education, and upper secondary education respectively (see Table 6). The table shows that Denmark's estimated relative efficiency is very low for this early period at around 0.5, a figure which is markedly below the level for the corresponding estimates for 2010 of 0.75-0.90 (see Table 7). The data underlying the results for Model 7 are presented in Figure 6, which also indicates the calculated production frontier. The graduation rate in Denmark was around 86 percent, the same as in 2010, but, relative to other countries, costs per student were much higher in Denmark in 2003 compared with 2010. In fact, Denmark and the USA had the highest levels of costs in 2003.

Table 13. Relative efficiencies from models where the output is graduation rates (in 2003) measured as the share of a birth cohort that completes a programme of education and input is costs per student (in 2000). Calculated for all countries (All) and Northern European countries (NE)

Model	7		8		9	
Countries	All	NE	All	NE	All	NE
Average	0.75	0.81	0.80	0.85	0.76	0.86
Denmark	0.50	0.50	0.53	0.53	0.48	0.48
Finland	0.75	0.75	0.78	0.78	0.85	0.85
Norway	1	1	1	1	0.59	1
Sweden	0.64	0.64	0.78	0.78	0.82	0.82
Germany	1*	1*	1*	1*	1*	1*
Ireland	1	1	1	1	1	1
Switzerland	0.56		0.62		0.64	
France	0.60		0.59		0.54	
Italy	0.61		0.66		0.65	
Greece	1*		1*		1	
Spain	0.81					
USA	0.50					

*Outlier

Figure 6. Graduation rates for upper secondary programmes in 2003 and PPP-corrected costs per student in primary and secondary education in 2000

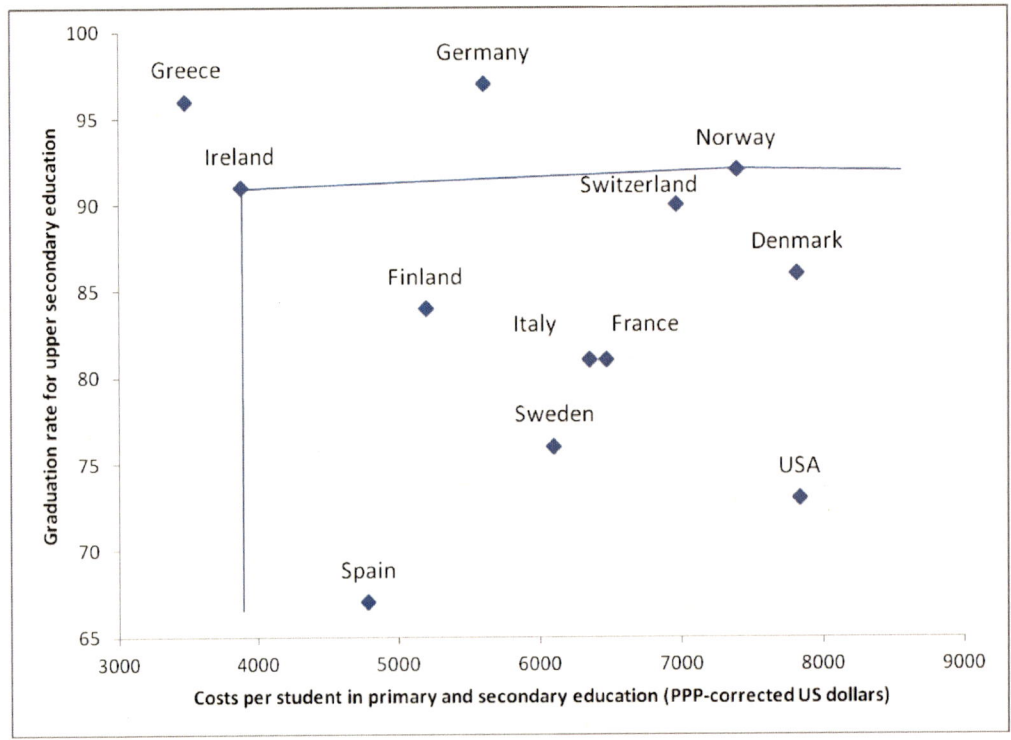

Table 14 shows the results for Models 24 and 25, in which the outputs are, respectively, expected earnings and expected earnings corrected for rate of employment for students completing an upper secondary programme in the year 2000, and the input is costs per student in primary and secondary education, again in 2000. Note that the calculations are based on the earnings and rate of employment in 2002, student numbers and costs in 2000, the graduation rate for tertiary education in 2003 and the completion rate for upper secondary education in 2010 (since this has not been calculated for earlier years). Denmark is an outlier in all the models, because it is the country with the highest expected earnings, also when corrected for rate of employment. Ireland is also an outlier; costs per student are very low there and expected earnings relatively high, so that Ireland has a great influence on the estimates of relative efficiency for a number of other countries. The data underlying the results are shown in Figures 7 and 8. Even though Denmark has higher costs per student than all of the other comparison countries, Denmark is completely efficient because of its high expected earnings after completion.

Around the year 2000, Denmark had higher costs per student than any of the other comparison countries except the USA, and the differences with other countries were greater than in 2010. Consequently, Denmark's estimated relative efficiency was lower in 2000 than in 2010, both in the quantitative models and in the models where graduation rate was the output. In models with expected earnings (or expected earnings corrected for employment rate) for students in upper secondary education as an indicator of quality, Denmark was completely efficient despite the high costs of education, because of the higher levels of expected earnings (also when corrected for rate of employment) than those in other countries. If Figures 7 and 8 are compared with Figures 4 and 5 respectively, it can be seen that expected earnings (with and without correction for rate of employment) were even higher in Denmark in around 2000 in comparison with other countries than was the case in around 2010.

Table 14. Relative efficiencies found in models where the output is earnings in 2002 or earnings in 2002 multiplied by rate of employment in 2002, and where the input is costs per student in primary and secondary education in 2000. Both inputs and outputs are PPP corrected. Calculations are made for all countries (All) and for Northern Europe (NE)

Model	24		25	
Output	Earnings		Earnings*rate of employment	
Countries	All	NE	All	NE
Average	0.95	0.97	0.96	0.99
Denmark	1*	1*	1*	1*
Finland	0.96	1	1	1
Norway	1	1	1	1
Sweden	0.78	0.85	0.96	0.96
Ireland	1*	1*	1*	1*
France	0.91		0.79	
Spain	1		1	

*Outlier

Figure 7. Relationships between expected future earnings for students in upper secondary education and average costs per student in primary and secondary education in 2000

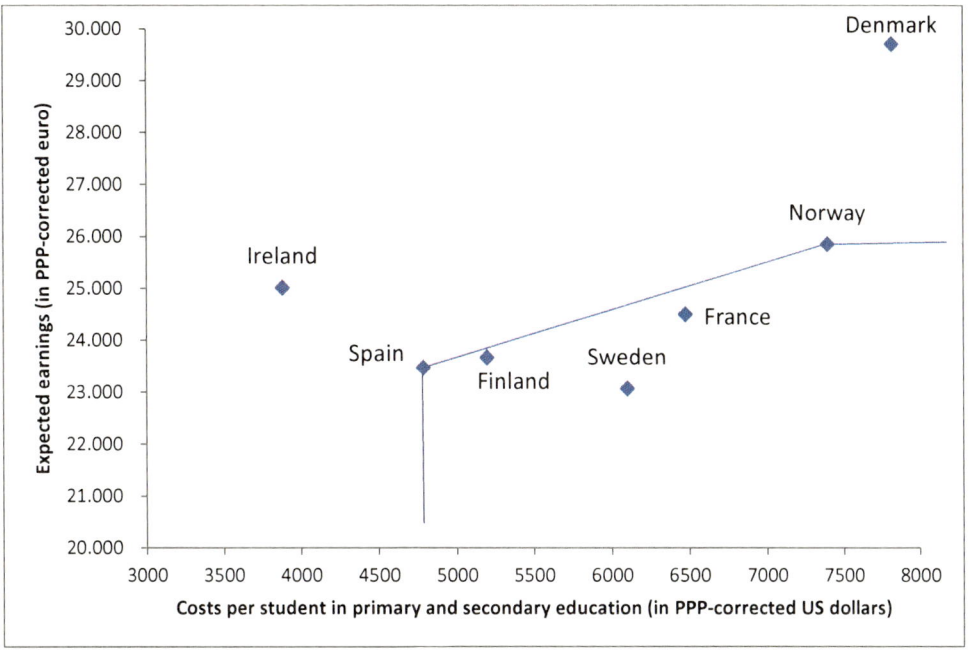

Figure 8. Relationships between expected future earnings for students in upper secondary education and average costs per student in primary and secondary education in 2000. Expected future earnings are calculated for various educational levels as annual earnings in 2002 multiplied by rate of employment in 2000

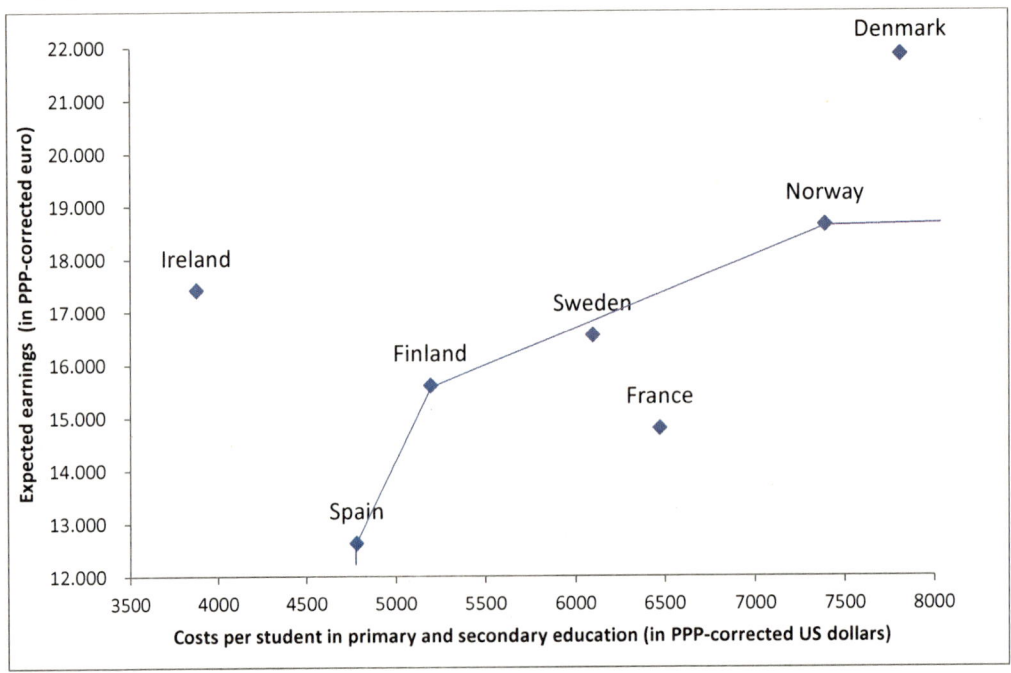

8. Summary and conclusions

Denmark, Norway, New Zealand, Canada and the USA are among the OECD nations that spend most on education – between 6.6 and 6.8 percent of GDP. However, spending priorities for the education budget vary greatly among these countries. Denmark, Norway and the USA expend a great deal on primary and lower secondary education, while Canada and New Zealand spend less on this area. In terms of costs per student, the USA is the country that spends by far the most on tertiary education. Denmark, Norway and Canada lie in the middle in this respect, with New Zealand spending least. By far the greatest share of expenditure on education in these countries comes from the public purse. Even in the USA, where private spending on education is greater than in the other countries, public expenditure on education still amounts to more than double the expenditure of private funds.

It is impossible to judge from these key figures alone whether educational production in a given country – Denmark, for example – is efficient, that is to say, whether the relationship between the numerous inputs to and outputs from educational production could not realistically be improved. Countries may have very different priorities with regard to the use of funds, for example in terms of the level in the education system which should be given the highest priority, and educational programmes may vary in quality from one country to another.

In order to get a step closer to being able to assess whether Denmark could improve the efficiency of its educational production, in particular with regard to upper secondary education, we have carried out a series of comparisons with best practice in a number of OECD countries, focusing particularly on countries from which it might be expected that Denmark could learn.

In the first analyses we focused on purely quantitative models in which total costs were measured against numbers of students. This was done, first, for all four levels of education (primary, lower secondary, upper secondary and tertiary); next, with the omission of tertiary education; then, without primary education, and the focus on secondary education alone; and finally, considering only upper secondary education. The reason for not focusing exclusively on upper secondary education was that we wished to test how robust the results were. There are significant differences among countries with regard to the structure of their education systems, including whether or not pupils are divided up onto different trajectories within an educational level, and there may – and probably will – be significant spillover effects between levels. The research method that we have chosen takes into account to some degree the uncertainties which these factors create.

The result found consistently in the analyses of the quantitative models is that Denmark could reduce its costs to some extent. When a large group of OECD countries is included in the analysis, the estimated potential savings for Denmark are between 12 and 37 percent, while the savings are rather less (between zero and nine percent) if Denmark is compared only to Northern European countries. Primary education is the most expensive level for Denmark relative to other countries. If we consider models focussing only on the secondary sector, Denmark's potential savings are between 12 and 27 percent when comparing to the large group of OECD countries, and between 3 and 9 percent when comparing to only Northern European countries. It is important to note that these results are based on models that take no account of qualitative aspects of the output. They only examine what it costs to educate students, not the results of this education.

Qualitative factors were subsequently taken into account in the study in several ways. First, we examined whether there was a positive correlation in general between low efficiency – i.e. high costs – and various indicators of high quality, including the share of those students who started course programmes who then completed them, the share of students who went on to study at a higher level, and the earnings that students who completed a programme could expect. On the whole, it was found that there was no significant correlation, neither positive nor negative. This is by no means an atypical result. One reason why high costs are not positively correlated with high quality is that systems that operate efficiently from the perspective of cost often perform well in other ways also, for example with respect to quality.

The second method that we used to incorporate indicators of the quality of education in the analyses was to include them as output in DEA models, where the central input was costs per student. In this part of the analysis we focused on graduation/completion rates and expected earnings after completion. In the models which only took into account graduation or completion rates for upper secondary education and costs per student, the estimated potential savings for Denmark were found to be 10-32 percent, depending on the definitions used of graduation/completion rate, cost variables, and the comparison group (restricting the comparison group to only Northern European countries, potential savings are 10-30 percent). Here, then, Denmark was found to be no more efficient than in the purely quantitative models, and less efficient actually in the more narrow Northern European comparison. This corresponds well with there being no positive correlation between quantitative efficiency and key qualitative indicators as mentioned above.

Nevertheless, Denmark's relative efficiency seems to have improved from 2000 to 2010. Thus, around the year 2000 Denmark's relative costs per student were much higher than in 2010, and in the purely quantitative models the estimated potential savings were 24-44 percent when comparing to Northern European countries. In the models with graduation rates in upper secondary education as outcome, potential savings were about 50 percent for all models and both comparison groups around year 2000. In these models, Denmark's improved efficiency from 2000 to 2010 are due to a reduction in relative costs per student, not higher graduation rates.

Even if Denmark's relative efficiency seems to have improved from 2000 to 2010, the Danish level of efficiency in 2010 seems rather low. Our analyses did shed some light on a factor which might help to explain Denmark's low efficiency level. We examined whether the scholastic skills which students brought to their upper secondary education might explain some of the inefficiency found. This did in fact prove to be the case. When countries' PISA scores are included, countries such as Denmark, Norway and Sweden, which perform relatively poorly on the PISA tests, make up ground on countries such as New Zealand and Finland, which perform well, and the differences in relative efficiency are then rather small. It seems reasonable to interpret this finding as an indication that the relatively low levels of efficiency in upper secondary education in the Scandinavian countries is due to students entering programmes at this level with a lower level of scholastic achievement than is the case in, for example, Finland and New Zealand. It should be noted, however, that in these analyses there was only a small number of observations relative to the number of variables, a factor which tends to result in higher estimates of relative efficiency.

The inclusion of expected earnings after completion of education for students in an upper secondary programme also shed light on the possible reasons for the low cost efficiency found for Denmark. In fact, these analyses suggest that perhaps Denmark is not inefficient at all, since Denmark was found to be completely efficient when expected future earnings for students enrolled in upper secondary education were included as output. However, a question mark does hang over the issue of whether this situation is stable, i.e. whether it is a stable and structural phenomenon that in Denmark, students enrolled in a programme of upper secondary education can expected to earn high wages, because the programmes are more productive than those in other countries, or whether it is an unstable phenomenon that may well disappear under the pressure of increased international competition. We examined this issue by checking the direction of the trend in recent years. There are indications that Denmark's position with very much higher earnings than other countries is in fact not stable. The expected earnings level (earnings multiplied by rate of employment) has fallen more in Denmark than in the other comparable countries. This trend may be linked to the economic cycle, in that Denmark has been hit especially hard by the economic crisis after 2008. In a slightly longer perspective, i.e. when we compare with the situation around the year 2000, our analyses show that earnings in Denmark have grown less quickly than in other countries, but at the same time that costs per student have also increased by relatively little in Denmark.

It is ultimately a political issue to determine whether high earnings for people with vocational training and for others who have completed upper secondary education is sufficiently important as a political objective to justify the high costs. In this context it could be useful to have available a number of different cost-benefit calculations in order to assist politicians in weighing up the options. However, such calculations are enormously complex, and the results unreliable. They would require very good methods of measuring the average benefits to society from the various levels of education, and thus they lie beyond the scope of the present analysis.

Appendix A. Frontier and best practice models

Institution models and the concept of efficiency

We can think of an educational institution as a production unit that transforms multiple inputs (resources) x into multiple outputs (products, services) y. We can call such an institution (or production unit) P^A, and can illustrate its operation as in Figure A1 below.

Figure A1. Simple model of an institution

Input might consist of, for example, teachers and other operating costs, while output could consist of numbers of students of various types.

x^A = (Teachers, Other operating costs)

y^A = (Type 1 students, Type 2 students)

In order to evaluate P^A we need a standard or a benchmark to measure it against.

In general, we can think of this standard as being the technology, T:

T = set of possible input/output combinations

In the next section we discuss how the technology can be estimated in practice.

The assessment of efficiency

When the technology is given, P^A can be assessed on the following logical basis. If it is possible to produce more output than y^A with fewer inputs than x^A, then P^A is inefficient. The amount of this inefficiency increases according to how much input could be saved without reducing the output, or according to how much the output could be increased without increasing the input.

This is illustrated in Figure A2.

In this figure, L(y) is the set of inputs which is sufficient to produce output y, while P(x) is the set of outputs that could be produced from input x. The frontiers of L and P are known as *isoquants*. L and P are simply an alternative way of describing the technology.

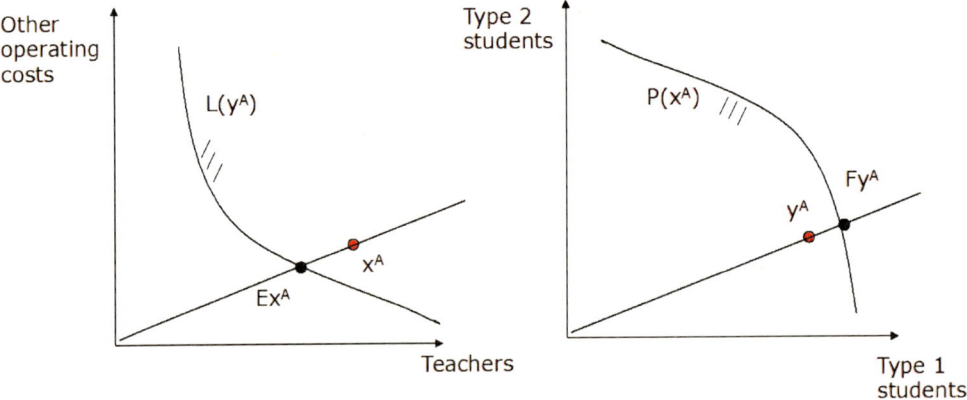

Figure A2. Farrell inefficiencies

We see that P^A uses more inputs than is strictly necessary. It would in fact be possible to reduce x^A to Ex^A and still have sufficient resources to produce the same level of output. This leads to the *Farrell measure of input efficiency*:

E = minimum input / actual input

Low values of E indicate large inefficiency – in other words, large potential for improvement. A score of, for example, $E = 0.7$ indicates that it would be possible to reduce inputs by 30 percent and still produce the current output.

Inefficiencies can also occur on the output side, when the current output using input x^A does not lie on the frontier of the production possibility set. In the illustration, it would actually be possible to increase output y^A to Fy^A using the current input resources x^A. This is the *Farrell measure of output efficiency*:

F = maximum output / actual current production

High values of F indicate large inefficiency – or, in other words again, large potential for improvement. A score of, for example, $F = 1.2$ indicates that it would be possible to increase output by 20 percent without increasing the current input.

Thus, the larger the distance between the actual production and the frontier of what the technology could achieve, the isoquant, the more inefficient is P^A. A large distance means that there is great potential for improvement.

We have described above how a specific institution's efficiency can be assessed theoretically. In order to apply these concepts in practice, however, it is necessary to have a model for the underlying technology, T. The technology is not described in any textbook; it must therefore be estimated on the basis of actual data. There are many ways of estimating technologies, and new ones are being developed all the time. We will not go into this area in detail in the present paper, but restrict ourselves to commenting on one or two central issues.

Frontier models and best practice

The basic idea in modern benchmarking is comparison with *best practice*. Best practice can be described as the best that it is possible to achieve in reality. Focusing on best practice has two consequences.

First, it means that we look at the maximum that can be achieved, as opposed to what the institutions concerned can achieve on average. This is in line with basic economic theory, where the technology or the production function describes the maximum that can be produced with a given input. This is something which should naturally be borne in mind when interpreting the results. It must also be remembered that not all institutions may be able to implement best practice, and that it may take time to actually implement best practice.

Second, choosing to estimate best practice means that we focus on the real world rather than on theoretical speculations. Instead of speculating about what could theoretically be achieved, we assess what real institutions have actually done. Best practice is not a single fixed benchmark or an ideal, but rather a description of the overall set of possibilities. In a benchmarking analysis, a systematic investigation is made at a suitable aggregated level of a large number of institutions.

Different approaches

The fundamental problem is that we cannot observe best practice directly. In the first instance, we can at best only show institutions in the form of simple data points, i.e. descriptions of the resources used and the services produced, and the local conditions under which production occurred. The main challenge is thus to create a model which can estimate the relationships between such data points representing actual observations. In brief, then, the problem is how to move from single observations (points) to a functional relationship as in Figure A3.

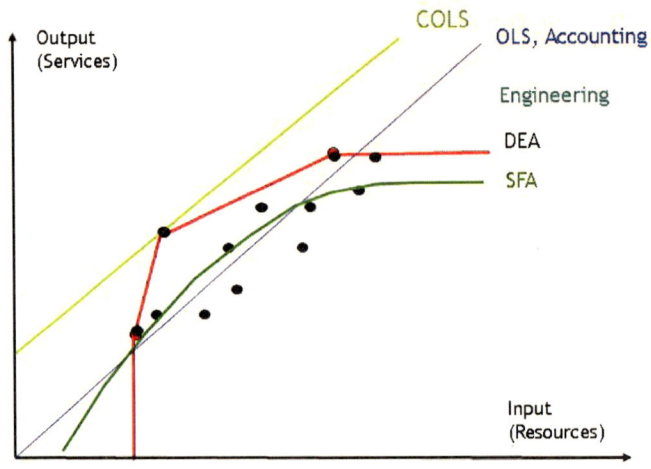

Figure A3. Alternative benchmark models

As the figure above indicates, there are several techniques available. These range from simple accounting methods and regression models through more advanced statistical and mathematical programming models to actual engineering-based or consultancy-based models of what it would cost if one designed a completely new institution.

In the literature, there is broad unanimity that there are basically four types of approach, as summarised in the taxonomy in Table A1.

	Deterministic	Stochastic
Parametric	Corrected Ordinary Least Squares (COLS)	Stochastic Frontier Analysis (SFA)
Non-parametric	Data Envelopment Analysis (DEA)	Stochastic Data Envelopment Analysis (SDEA)

Table A1. A benchmarking taxonomy

The parametric models assume a certain functional format from the outset, and use data to calibrate the parameters in that format. A significant advantage of the non-parametric methods is that they make fewer *a priori* assumptions concerning the possible relationships between costs and services. They make only very general assumptions, for examples that costs increase with the level of service. The advantage of the parametric models, on the other hand, is that they make it easier to separate noise in the data from real inefficiency.

The most widely used methods in practice are *Data Envelopment Analysis (DEA)* and *Stochastic Frontier Analysis (SFA)*, which are also clearly the most theoretically useful models when advantages and disadvantages are weighed up.

DEA methods

In this paper, we have primarily made use of DEA methods.

Data Envelopment Analysis (DEA) was originally put forward by Charnes, Cooper and Rhodes (1978, 79), and has subsequently been further developed in a great many articles. Bogetoft and Otto (2011) is an up-to-date, technically-oriented textbook in the field, while Bogetoft (2012) provides a more management-oriented presentation. Other textbooks include Coelli *et al.* (2008) and Cooper *et al.* (2008).

These methods have internationally been used for productivity assessments of, for example, schools, universities, hospitals, military units, post offices, police forces and banks. In Denmark, too, the methods have been used by ministries and consultants within a variety of areas. The first applications in Denmark concerned evaluations of research institutions and hospitals; see Jennergren and Obel (1986) and Bogetoft, Olesen and Petersen (1987). The Danish Ministry of Finance produced an introduction in Danish to benchmarking methods and DEA in particular, discussing them in connection with a number of applications including primary/lower secondary schools, hospitals, care of the elderly, and the police (Finansministeriet 2000).

Emrouznejad *et al.* (2008) is a very comprehensive bibliography covering the first 30 years of development of DEA. More than 4,000 scientific applications of DEA are identified, published in journals or as book chapters. A list of publications can be found at www.deazone.com. Counting PhD theses, working papers, etc. there were more than 7,000 relevant publications in existence by 2007, some discussing various theoretical aspects of the method, others various practical applications. The most widespread areas of application appear to be within the fields of banking, finance, education and healthcare. A large number of European countries now use DEA models to set reasonable income restrictions, for example for regulated energy network companies.

DEA is based on the principle of *minimal extrapolation*. The idea is that one takes data from other institutions, and attempts to extrapolate as little as possible from these data and yet arrive at some comparisons. In technical terms, this means finding the smallest number of input/output combinations that contain the actual observations, and which fulfil a small number of supplementary assumptions. We will now consider some of the commonest of these supplementary assumptions.

The most frequently used is the assumption of the *free disposability of inputs and outputs*. This means that if an institution has the same amount or more of all resources as at present, it can produce at least the same amount of services; and if the institution is required to produce fewer services, then the old level of resources is the maximum that will be required.

Another common assumption is that of *convexivity*. In practice, this means that if there are two institutions, it is assumed that it is possible to create weighted averages of these; in other words, that we can construct a pseudo-institution which, for example, uses 25 percent of Institution 1's total input plus 75 percent of that of Institution 2, and produces 25 percent of Institution 1's output plus 75 percent of that of Institution 2. Convexivity is a slightly more technical assumption, but it is one which is normally included in economics models.

Last but not least, it is often assumed that it is meaningful to scale a unit up or down. There are four standard assumptions concerning *returns to scale*:

CRS (constant returns to scale) means that an institution can be freely scaled up and down. If for example 25 percent of current resources are used, it will still be possible to produce 25 percent of current services, and if resources are doubled, then output of services can also be doubled.

DRS (decreasing returns to scale) means that it is possible to scale down but not necessarily to scale up, because there may be certain disadvantages to being large.

IRS (increasing returns to scale) means that it is possible to scale up but not necessarily to scale down, because there may be certain disadvantages to being small (e.g. fixed costs).

VRS (variable returns to scale) means that in principle it is not possible to scale up or down.

Figure A4 shows a hypothetical case in which five institutions, A-E, are given, each described in terms of one input and one output. Depending on the assumptions made, we obtain different estimates of the underlying technology, and therefore also different estimates of the possibilities for improvement. In an FDH model we only assume the free disposability of inputs and outputs. This means that Institutions A, E, B and C all lie on the frontier of the technology and thus represent best practice. Only Institution D could improve, i.e. reduce input, increase output, or both. If we introduce convexity, the FDH model becomes the VRS model. This shows that E can also improve, and that D can improve more than was indicated previously. In DRS we can also scale down; we can scale up in IRS and both scale up and scale down in CRS. In the last case it is only Institution B which cannot be improved. The last technology, FRH (free replicability hull), is based on the assumption that it is possible to replicate and *add together* units. If, for example, it is possible to operate an institution as A and as B, it is assumed that it is also possible to operate an institution as 2*A+B – i.e. that the large institution can be split into three divisions, two structured in the same way as A and one in the same way as B.

The choice of returns to scale can be made on the basis of various premises.

It is possible to use statistical tests and thus let the data determine how scale actually influences the returns. We can, for example, compare the efficiency levels in successive steps as more return to scale possibilities are introduced one by one, and reject the extra assumptions if the efficiency levels fall significantly.

One can also argue for the choice of return to scale assumptions by logical and conceptual deduction. It could, for example, be argued that IRS makes more sense than DRS, in that if a unit is too big, as can happen in DRS, it should in principle be possible to reorganise the institution internally – for example, by establishing two independent divisions – thus eliminating or at least significantly reducing any disadvantages of operating on a large scale.

The issue can also be considered from a motivational or regulatory perspective. In this context, it could be said that the sector should strive for an optimum size, where the unit costs are as low as possible – and this is precisely what happens if inefficiencies are reduced in a CRS model.

In this paper, statistical texts and conceptual deduction are the methods primarily used to select returns to scale.

A more technical discussion of DEA methods can be found at the end of this Appendix.

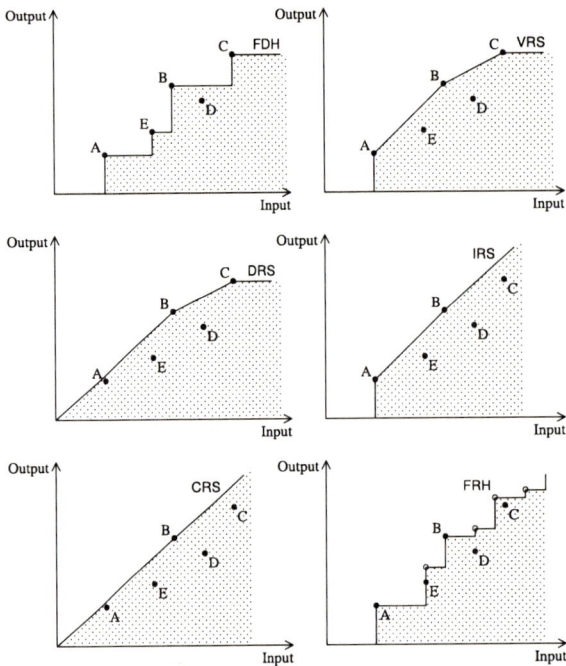

Figure A4. Various DEA models in simple cases with one input and one output

Outliers

A particular challenge in using benchmarking models, from both theoretical and practical points of view, is the elimination of *outliers*.

Since benchmarking models aim to estimate what is best practice, they are relatively sensitive to single observations. It is therefore important to have good outlier identification techniques, and following the principle of caution, to apply aggressive outlier elimination.

Outliers are removed through thorough data checks. Various econometric methods, such as the use of Cook's distance estimates, can be of value in making such checks on the data and in identifying any countries that should not be included in the estimation because they would have too great an influence on the final result. A number of methods have been developed for identifying frontier outliers in connection with best practice models. The first is based on Banker's super-efficiency procedure (see Banker and Chang, 2006). Let $E(k;I)$ be the efficiency of a country k when it is compared with best practice in all countries I, and let $E(k;I\backslash i)$ be the efficiency of country k when it is compared with best practice in all countries I except for country i. If the super-efficiency $E(i;I\backslash i)$ of a country i is very high compared to that of other countries, this country will normally be considered an outlier. We use a specific condition in the analyses, described in Bogetoft and Otto as the German condition, namely to regard a country as an outlier if it is above the so-called upper fence

$$E(i;I\backslash i) > q(0.75) + 1.5*(q(0.75)-q(0.25))$$

where $q(0.25)$ and $q(0.75)$ are the 25 percent and 75 percent fractiles in the distribution of super-efficiencies, i.e. 25 percent of countries have a super-efficiency below $q(0.25)$ and 75 percent have a super-efficiency below $q(0.75)$. This criterion thus eliminates countries with very high super-efficiencies. Another criterion is based on Banker's F test. The idea is to eliminate those countries which seem to affect the relative efficiencies of other countries to a very great degree. This is done by considering the statistical indicator

$$\sum_{k \in I\backslash i}(E(k;I\backslash i) - 1)^2 / \sum_{k \in I\backslash i}(E(k;I) - 1)^2$$

Low values for this indicator mean that many countries would seem considerably more efficient if the model were estimated without country i. How low the values should be to be statistically significant is determined by using the fact that the indicator is asymmetrically distributed, $F(n-1,n-1)$ where n is the number of observations (countries) (Banker 1996). Values below, for example, the five percent fractile in this distribution would lead to excluding country i from the estimation. Other methods also exist, including calculating the volume of the data and determining which institutions particularly expand it (Wilson, 1993), but the methods described above are particularly intuitive and they are therefore used in all the analyses of this paper.

Bootstrapping and bias correction

Another challenge that is particularly relevant in relation to this paper is the *bias problem*. DEA models estimate an inner approximation of the production possibilities and create what are from the outset over-optimistic evaluations of the efficiencies of institutions. The problem is that the biases in the evaluations are not necessarily the same for all institutions. The bias is greatest when there are few comparable institutions, and that is a problem, because ideally we would wish to use peer institutions as a comparison group. Institutions for which there exist only small comparison groups will thus be more likely to be evaluated as efficient than institutions for which there are large comparison groups, just as, all else being equal, it is easier to win a competition when there are few participants than when there are many.

There are, however, solidly-grounded methods whereby this problem of bias can be reduced. The most common is to *bootstrap* the efficiency values. This allows the bias to be estimated, and bias-corrected confidence intervals can then be constructed.

DEA technology

In the remainder of this appendix we present a more precise description of the DEA technologies used.

In classical production economics, an *institution* is defined as a unit that converts one or more inputs into one or more outputs under given conditions. The possibilities for transforming inputs into outputs define the *production possibility set* or the *technology*. The production possibility set describes the possible combinations of input and output:

$$T=\{(x,y): x \text{ can produce } y\}$$

where x is an m-dimensional input vector and y is an n-dimensional output vector. In practice, the technology is not known, and must therefore be estimated.

DEA methods estimate T on the basis of a number of observed production input/output combinations (x^j, y^j), i.e. $j=1,...,J$ institutions, and on the basis of certain minimal assumptions concerning what a real-life production possibility set should be like. The estimate of T is the *empirical reference technology*, and in the following this will be designated T^*. One characteristic of DEA methods is that T^* is constructed on the basis of the *minimal extrapolation principle*:

T^* is the smallest subset of R_o^{m+n} that contains the observed productions (x^j, y^j), $j=1,...,J$, and which fulfils certain technological assumptions (see below).

It follows from this principle that if T fulfils the technological assumptions, then T^* will be an inner approximation of T, i.e. $T^* \subseteq T$. This means that if an institution's performance is evaluated in relation to T^* instead of to the true technology T, the result will be a cautious or conservative estimate of the institution's inefficiencies. One precondition for this, however, is that the data should be of good quality; the method does not take possible flaws in the data into account. We have therefore introduced various additional steps, in particular outlier elimination, in this paper.

The most common technological assumption in DEA-like methods is the assumption of *free disposability*:

A1: $(x,y) \in L, x' \geq x, y' \leq y \Rightarrow (x',y') \in T$

which means that it is assumed that it is always possible to dispose of surplus inputs and outputs, or that it is always possible to produce less with more.

Another frequent assumption is the *assumption of convexity*:

A2: $(x,y) \in T, (x',y') \in Y, \alpha \in [0,1] \Rightarrow \alpha(x,y)+(1-\alpha)(x',y') \in T$

which states that the number of feasible production possibilities is convex. This and other similar assumptions of convexity are widely used in economic theory, but they are naturally not always unproblematic in empirical analyses.

A final group of common assumptions are the *assumptions of returns to scale*:

$$A3(k): (x,y) \in T \Rightarrow \alpha(x,y) \in T \quad \forall \alpha \in K(k)$$

where k=crs, drs, irs or vrs, and where $K(crs) = R_o$, $K(drs) = [0,1]$, $K(irs) = [1,\infty)$ and $K(vrs) = \{1\}$. *A3(crs)*, where crs stands for *constant returns to scale*, states that it is possible to freely upscale or downscale production. *A3(drs)*, where drs stands for *decreasing returns to scale*, states that it is always possible to downscale production. *A3(irs)*, where irs stands for *increasing returns to scale*, states that it is always possible to downscale production. *A3(vrs)* means that no assumptions are made regarding upscaling or downscaling. More precisely, vrs stands for *varying returns to scale*; it means that returns to scale can vary according to which output production we consider. Return to scale is a common concept in economics, and concerns how quickly output increases with input in efficient production. Global assumptions of returns to scale are used in DEA. In the case of one input and one output, constant returns to scale means that every additional unit of input gives rise to the same quantity of additional output. Diminishing returns to scale means that the output effect of additional input diminishes (disadvantages of scale), while increasing returns to scale means that additional units of input give rise to increasing amounts of output (advantages of scale).

A special type of return to scale can be modelled under the assumption of *additivity*:

$$A3(add): (x,y) \in T, (x',y') \in T \Rightarrow (x+x', y+y') \in T$$

This means that if two input/output combinations are each possible, then the sum of them is also possible. This assumption is rarely used, since it leads to analyses which require a great deal of calculation. Additivity is, however, a naturally intuitive assumption, since large institutions can easily be conceived as comprising independent divisions.

Different DEA methods are based on the use of different technological assumptions. It is easy to see that the minimal extrapolation principle combined with these assumptions leads to the *empirical reference technology* below:

$$T^*(k) = \{(x,y) \in R_o^{m+n}: \exists \lambda \in R_o^J: x \geq \Sigma_j \lambda^j x^j, y \leq \Sigma_j \lambda^j y^j, \lambda \in \Lambda(k)\}$$

where $\Lambda(crs) = R_o^J$, $\Lambda(drs) = \{\lambda \in R_o^J: \Sigma_j \lambda^j \leq 1\}$, $\Lambda(irs) = \{\lambda \in R_o^J: \Sigma_j \lambda^j \geq 1\}$, $\Lambda(vrs) = \{\lambda \in R_o^n: \Sigma_j \lambda^j = 1\}$, $\Lambda(fdh) = \{\lambda \in \{0,1\}^J: \Sigma_j \lambda^j = 1\}$, and $\Lambda(add) = \{0,1,2,3..\}^J$.

In benchmarking analyses, the efficiency of a given institution is evaluated in terms of the distance from the frontier of the production possibility set, i.e. the distance from best practice. This distance can be measured in many ways, but the dominant method in the literature is the use of *Farrell's efficiencies*. Farrell's input efficiency, typically designated E, measures the maximum proportional reductions of all inputs which would still permit production of current output if best practice were adopted. Similarly, Farrell's output efficiency, typically designated F, is the maximum proportional increase in all outputs which would be possible with the given inputs if best practice were adopted.

Since the true technology T is not known but only estimated as T^*, it is normal to speak of the *relative efficiency*, since we are talking about efficiency relative to that of the other institutions we have used to estimate the technology. If we designate the relative efficiency scores in the input and output spaces as E^* and F^* respectively, the efficiency scores can be defined as:

$$E^{*i} = \min\{E \in R_o: (Ex^i, y) \in T^*\} \text{ and } F^{*i} = \max\{F \in R_o: (x^i, Fy^i) \in T^*\}$$

When we use DEA estimates of T^*, the relative efficiencies can be found by solving simple linear programming (LP) problems, provided that we confine ourselves to vrs, drs, irs and crs models. For example, $E^{*i}(k)$ can be calculated by solving the following LP problem:

Minimise: E

Subject to: $Ex^i \geq \Sigma_j \lambda^j x^j$

$y^i \leq \Sigma_j \lambda^j y^j$

$\lambda \in \Lambda(k), E \geq 0$

$E^{*i}(k)$ here expresses the amount by which all of Institution i's inputs can be reduced if the institution is to continue to produce at least the same quantity of output. This is done in the programming model by calculating a combination of all the input/output vectors of comparable institutions which minimise input and still produce at least the same output y^i. In the case of *fdh* and *add* models, the process involved is a little more complex than solving simple LP problems. In the *fdh* case, the problem can be solved relatively easily by simply going through all the potential solutions. In the *add* case, however, it is necessary to use an integer programming algorithm.

Similarly, we can calculate $F^{*i}(k)$ by solving an LP (or mixed integer) problem:

Maximise: F

Subject to: $x^i \geq \Sigma_j \lambda^j x^j$

$Fy^i \leq \Sigma_j \lambda^j y^j$

$\lambda \in \Lambda(k), F \geq 0$

$F^{*i}(k)$ expresses the amount by which we can increase all Institution i's output while maintaining a combination of input/output which does not use more input and which produces at least the same output. The F^i programme has the same number of variables and conditions as the E^i programme.

An interesting alternative interpretation of these DEA programmes emerges from the *dual optimisation problem*. This dual problem introduces prices (or weights) into the input and output, and the solution to the dual problem comprises the prices which result in optimal production from the unit being evaluated. This allows us to argue that the relative efficiency score is a pessimistic measure of the potential for improvement of an institution.

Appendix B. Calculation methods and data for the four indicators of quality

1. Graduation rates (completion rates in relation to the *population*)
    - In the case of upper secondary education, this rate is measured as the share of a birth cohort of the relevant age that completes a programme of secondary education. In the OECD's data, this is calculated by dividing the number of students who graduate from upper secondary education in a given year (2010) by the total number of people in the population of the typical age for completion of upper secondary education (OECD 2012, Annex 3, p. 23). The calculation is inevitably affected by the fact that there may be great variation in the actual age of people graduating from upper secondary education and in the size of age cohorts.
    - In the case of tertiary education, this rate is measured as the share of a birth cohort of the relevant age made up of students who graduate *for the first time* from a programme of tertiary education, regardless of the age at which they graduate. The calculation is based on the number of students graduating from a programme of tertiary education in a given year (2010) and their age distribution (OECD 2013, p. 55). There is a special problem in calculating the graduation rate for tertiary education with respect to overseas students. If a large proportion of the young people in a given country take their tertiary education in a foreign country, the graduation rate will be an underestimate (e.g. in the case of Luxembourg), whereas it will be an overestimate in the case of a country such as the UK, where the number of overseas students is high (even calculated net of UK students going abroad to study).

2. Completion rates (the share of the students *who started a programme* who go on to complete it)
    - Upper secondary programmes: For over half the countries in the study, the completion rate for upper secondary education was calculated using a true cohort method, i.e. students who began an upper secondary programme in a given year were followed up on an individual basis to discover how many completed the programme within its normal duration, and within the normal duration plus two years. For the remaining countries, the completion rate was calculated as the number of students completing an upper secondary programme in a given year (2010) divided by the number who began the programme N years previously, where N is the normal duration of the programme (OECD 2012, Annex 3, pp 27-8). This method of calculation takes into account changes in the size of the relevant age cohort, but does not take into account whether or not students completed the programme within the normal time.
    - Tertiary education: For around half the countries in the study, the completion rates were calculated using a true cohort method. All the individuals who began a tertiary programme in a given year were traced, and it was determined how many had later completed that or another programme of tertiary education. For the remaining countries, the completion rate was calculated as the number of students completing a

tertiary programme in a given year (2011) divided by the number who began the programme N years previously, where N is the normal duration of the programme (OECD 2013, p. 70).

3. The earnings rates used in the main analysis are for 2010 and are based on data from Eurostat (Eurostat 2014: Dataset earn_ses10_30). Earnings for each of the three levels are based on average earnings for people in employment with ISCED educational levels 0-2, 3-4 and 5-6 (where, for example, the distribution of the population across levels 3 and 4 provides the basis for combining the earnings for level 3 and for level 4). More precisely, the expected earnings for students in upper secondary education (EUS) are determined as:

$$EUS = (1 - CRUS) * E02 + CRUS * (1 - GRT)E34 + CRUS * GRT * E56$$

where $CRUS$ is the completion rate for upper secondary level; $E02$, $E34$ and $E56$ are, respectively, average earnings for individuals with compulsory schooling, upper secondary education and tertiary education as their highest completed educational level; and GRT is the graduation rate for tertiary education related to students in upper secondary level (i.e. graduation rate tertiary / graduation rate upper secondary).

4. The rates of employment used are based on Eurostat (2014: Dataset lfsa_ergaed) and in the main analysis are an average for the years 2007-12. In a supplementary analysis in the study, the rates are based on data for 2012 alone. Expected earnings are corrected for rates of employment calculated in the same way as EUS above, except that the earnings for the various levels of education ($E02$, $E34$ are $E56$) are replaced by earnings multiplied by rate of employment for the corresponding educational level, i.e. $E02*emp02$, $E34*emp34$ and $E56*emp56$, where $emp02$, $emp34$ and $emp56$ are rates of employment.

References

Afonso, António and Miguel St. Aubyn (2005). 'Non-parametric approaches to education and health efficiency in OECD countries', *Journal of Applied Economics*, 8 (2): 227-246.

Afonso, António and Miguel St. Aubyn (2006). 'Cross-country efficiency of secondary education provision – A semi-parametric analysis with non-discretionary inputs', *Economic Modelling*, 23 (3): 476-491.

Andersen, Lotte Bøgh, Peter Bogetoft, Jørgen Grønnegård Christensen and Torben Tranæs (eds) (2014). *Styring, ledelse og resultater på ungdomsuddannelserne*. Odense: Rockwool Fondens Forskningsenhed and Syddansk Universitetsforlag.

Banker, Rajiv D. (1996). 'Hypothesis tests using Data Envelopment Analysis', *Journal of Productivity Analysis*, 7 (2-3): 139-160.

Banker, Rajiv D. and Hsihui Chang (2006). 'The super-efficiency procedure for outlier identification, not for ranking efficient units', *European Journal of Operational Research*, 175 (2): 1311-1320.

Bogetoft, Peter (2012). *Performance Benchmarking – Measuring and Managing Performance*. New York: Springer.

Bogetoft, Peter, Eskil Heinesen and Torben Tranæs (2014). *Internationale effektivitetsforskelle i uddannelsesproduktion*. Study Paper. Copenhagen: Rockwool Fondens Forskningsenhed.

Bogetoft, Peter, Ole Olesen and Niels Christian Petersen (1987). 'Produktivitetsevaluering af 96 danske sygehuse – En præsentation af DEA-metoden og et eksempel på dens anvendelse', *Ledelse og Erhvervsøkonomi*, 51 (2): 67-81.

Bogetoft, Peter and Lars Otto (2011). *Benchmarking with DEA, SFA, and R*. New York: Springer.

Bogetoft, Peter og Jesper Wittrup (2014). 'Effektive skoler: Benchmarking af danske ungdomsud- dannelsesinstitutioner med særligt fokus på gymnasierne', Chapter 7 in Andersen *et al.* (2014).

Charnes, A., W.W. Cooper and E. Rhodes (1978). '*Measuring the efficiency of decision making units*', *European Journal of Operational Research*, 2: 429-444.

Charnes, A., W.W. Cooper and E. Rhodes (1979). 'Short communication: *Measuring the efficiency of decision making units*', *European Journal of Operational Research*, 3: 339.

Christensen, Flemming, Peter Fristrup and Jens Leth Hougaard (1991). *Produktivitetsanalyser*. Copenhagen: Jurist- og Økonomforbundets Forlag.

Coelli, Timothy, D.S. Prasada Rao, Christopher J. O'Donnell and George E. Battese (2008). *An Introduction to Efficiency and Productivity Analysis*. New York: Springer.

Cooper William W., Lawrence M. Seiford and Kaoru Tone (2007). *Data Envelopment Analysis: A Comprehensive Text with Models, Applications, References and DEA-Solver Software*, 2nd edn. New York: Springer.

DEA (2013). *International sammenligning af erhvervsuddannelser*, DEA-rapport 13/05/2013. Copenhagen: Tænketanken DEA.

Deprins, D., D. Simar, and H. Tulkens (1984). '*Measuring labor efficiency in post offices*', pp. 243-267 in M. Marchand, P. Pestieau, and H. Tulkens, *The Performance of Public Enterprises: Concepts and Measurements*. Amsterdam: North-Holland.

Emrouznejad, Ali, Barnett R. Parker and Gabriel Tavares (2008). 'Evaluation of research in efficiency and productivity: A survey and analysis of the first 30 years of scholarly literature in DEA', *Journal of Socio-Economics Planning Science*, 42 (3k): 151- 157.

Eurostat (2014). Eurostats database, http://epp.eurostat.ec.europa.eu/portal/page/portal/statistics/search_database. Data for lønninger og beskæftigelsesgrader opdelt efter uddannelse. Accessed January-April 2014.

Finansministeriet (2000). *Benchmarking i den offentlige sektor – nogle metoder og erfaringer*. Copenhagen: Finansministeriet.

Jennergren, L. Peter and Børge Obel (1986). 'Forskningsevaluering – eksemplificeret ved 22 økonomiske institutter', *Økonomi and Politik*, 59 (2): 86-95.

Markussen, Eifred (ed.) (2010). 'Frafall i utdanning for 16-20 åringer i Norden', *TemaNord 2010: 517*. Copenhagen: Nordisk Ministerråd.

OECD (2012). *Education at a Glance 2012*.

OECD (2013). *Education at a Glance 2013*.

Verhoeven, Marijn, Victoria Gunnarsson and Stéphane Carcillo (2007). *Education and Health in G7 Countries: Achieving Better Outcomes with Less Spending*, IMF Working Paper WP/07/263. International Monetary Fund.